D0384024

READY TO LIVE, PREPARED TO DIE

Amy Harwell

Ready to Live

Prepared to Die

A Provocative Guide to the Rest of Your Life

Wheaton, Illinois
Harold Shaw Publishers

Copyright © 1995 by Amy Harwell

Unless otherwise indicated, all Scripture quotations are taken from *The Holy Bible: New International Version*. Copyright © 1973, 1978, 1984 by the International Bible Society. Used by permission of Zondervan Publishing House. All rights reserved.

All rights reserved. No part of this book may be reproduced or transmitted in any form or by any means, electronic or mechanical, including photocopying, recording, or any information storage and retrieval system without written permission from Harold Shaw Publishers, Box 567, Wheaton, Illinois 60189. Printed in the United States of America.

Cover design by David LaPlaca

Cover photo © 1995 by Karen Woodburn

ISBN 0-87788-704-7

Library of Congress Cataloging-in-Publication Data

Harwell, Amy.
   Ready to live, prepared to die : a provocative guide to the rest of your life / Amy Harwell.
     p. cm.
   Includes bibliographical references.
   ISBN 0-87788-704-7 (pbk.)
   1. Death—Religious aspects—Christianity. 2. Harwell, Amy. 3. Cancer—Patients—United States—Biography. 4. Christian biography—United States.
I. Title.
   BT825.H33 1995
   248.8'6—dc20   94—12462
                                               CIP

---

02 01 00 99 98 97 96 95

10 9 8 7 6 5 4 3 2 1

I dedicate this book to Andrea S. DesCoteaux,
a constant Caleb.

With a grateful heart for

Polly Aschom, a loving Luke
Rae Ellsworth, a gracious Gabriel
Melinda and Gordon Hinners, modest Barnabases
Kaye Vivian, a sensitive scribe
and
Jayne and Jess Harwell, my parents,
who understand my purpose in sharing these
most personal reflections and beliefs so publicly.

Inspire me with the spirit of joy and gladness;
and make me the cup of strength to suffering souls.
—*Forward Day by Day*

Acknowledgments

For those saints—both the living and the dead—who encouraged, questioned, supported, challenged, and prayed for me and this book. Thank you.

Logan Aschom	Louise Erpelding	Karen Kellow	Allan Renz
Tom Aschom	Suzanne Evans	Jim Kelly	Jim Rehnberg
Paul Avakian	Mary Evins	Marilou Kelly	Margy Rehnberg
Shirley Avakian	Andrew Fauntleroy	Tom King	Greg Risberg
Richard Baer	Patrick Fauntleroy	Janet Lang	Patty Rossiter
Pam Ballantine	Flannel	David LaPlaca	Eugene Ruark
Pat Bango	Joe Fouts	Ray Lang	Sally Ruark
Sheri Bango	Nancy Fouts	Susan Leigh	Guy Sas
Gary Behrends	Bill Gallagher	Donna Lobs	Tracy Sas
Carolyn Berg	Lou Gallagher	Rick Lobs	Leonard Schram
Paula Berg	Diane Gibson	Dan Lupton	Luci Shaw
Steve Board	Harvey Gilman	Bob MacNeille	Bobbie Smith
Joan Borysenko	Andrew Glass	Diane MacNeille	Paula Smith
Judy Brannon	Mary Glass	David Mains	Melva Soderlund
Maureen	Gordon Gregory	Karen Mains	Dan Stovall
Broderick	Mary Gregory	Wally Malone	Carol Swenson
Fred Brunner	Marilyn Griffin	Patti Marks	Reg Swenson
Mary Brunner	Joan Guest	Martin Marty	Judy Tatelbaum
Barbara Aschom	Lisa Gunkel	Matthew	Teddy
Camara	Mary Haggard	Bruce Meiloch	John Temple
Daouda Camara	Joyce Harper	Judy Meiloch	Dick Temple
Teresa Camozzi	Robert Henry	Randall Millikan	Nancy Temple
Jana Carpenter	Fred Hoffman	Gail Muranyi	Nancy Ellen
Ruth Cornell	Sandy Hoffman	Emma Myer	Temple
Gordon Craft	Nancy Hollmeier	Pam Nelson	Michele Thatcher
Janet Craft	Ron Hollmeier	Vivian Nimmo	Nicholas Thorpe
Pat Crull	Evon Jarvis	Joyce Normandeau	Ulla Thorpe
Frank Cummings	Howard Jessen	Barbara O'Connell	Ramona Tucker
Carrie Curtain-	Susie Jessen	Laurence	Lori Turek
Rath	Judy Johnson	O'Connell	Fran Tynan
Jack D'Arcy	Tom Johnston	Lloyd Ogilvie	Ken Vaux
Meg D'Arcy	Peggy Jordan	Jim Otepka	Gordon Warren
Linda Darling	Joshua	Gaius Overton	Jim Warren
Sue Dawson	Gil Juern	Betsy Penny	Judith Warren
Paul DesCoteaux	Melba Juern	Susan Person	George Wilbanks
Terry DesCoteaux	Jim Kackley	Precious	Barbara
Karen Dingfelder	Bobbie Kallstrom	Bonnie Pritchard	Wischmeier
Bill Ellsworth	Charlie Kallstrom	Jim Pritchard	Vinita Wright
Linda Erpelding	Deborah Keisler	Chris Purdie	

Contents

Preface

Dear Reader . . .

This book is about *living!* It is about living in the *precious present moment!* This book is about living the precious present moment *joyfully!*

However, this book is also about the difficult journey and challenges toward this goal.

Let me share a true story.

Having read *When Your Friend Gets Cancer: How You Can Help*, my first book, the rental manager of my apartment building asked me to talk with another woman who was experiencing serious cancer. Ironically, of all the units in a fifty-two-story building, Patti lived directly across from me. Our lifestyles and work patterns were markedly different, and we had never met.

After our first introduction, Patti and I would call and visit each other periodically and support each other on our respective journeys. My earlier cancer had spread. Now we both had tumors in our lungs. Patti's cancer was more advanced than mine. Mine was just developing.

During a time when she was out of the hospital and back home, and on an evening when she felt like going out, we had a wonderful Italian meal together. Returning to our building that night, Patti stopped on a curbside, reached for my arm, and turned her frail body and stated, "Amy, you have something that I don't have. You seem to be at peace. What's your secret?"

The "secret" was simply this: I had worked through my dying to go on with my living. I believe that once we have prepared to die, we are really freed to live in whatever time we have left. Patti died shortly after our conversation. It's too late to give this book to Patti, but I know she'd like me to share it with you.

Introduction:
Called to Take
the Final Journey

"She doesn't know." It was my mother's voice I
heard as I woke groggily from surgery. I opened my
eyes and looked into the face of the psychiatrist, a
member of the cancer team. My cancer had spread to
my lymph system and was much more serious than
any of us had allowed ourselves to think.

"I'm going to die." This time it was my own voice.
I remember vividly saying those words a few days
later in the hospital. I had walked down the corridor
to the end of the hall, with my father silently at my side,
to the floor-to-ceiling picture window displaying the
sweeping vista of the entire Chicago skyline. It was the
first time this reality hit home; I finally realized that I
was, indeed, a mortal being. I finally understood that
I would die. I was thirty-five years old.

It was as if I heard a faint announcement from an
overhead speaker, "Calling all passengers!" Have you
heard the same faint long-distance call? It's the call to
take our final journey.

Are you facing a life-threatening event of your
own? Or of someone you love? Perhaps you, too, have
cancer, or maybe heart disease, advanced diabetes, or
AIDS. Maybe you want to prepare in case of an accident. Or maybe you feel that it's the season of your life
when shadows lengthen, when it's time to think about

dying. Our routes and our transports vary, but we now hear that subtle beckoning to begin the journey.

This announcement shouldn't be news; death is all around us. Our gardens are harvested; our fall leaves are raked. Goldfish and gerbils are buried with ceremony; maybe friends and family have been, too. The book of Ecclesiastes reminds us that everything happens in this world at the time God chooses:

> *He sets the time for birth*
> *and sets the time for death, . . .*
> *He sets the time for sorrow*
> *and the time for joy, . . .*
> *He sets the time for finding,*
> *and the time for losing.*
> —adapted from Ecclesiastes 3:2-5

I suddenly became aware that we are *all* both living and dying, every day, every year. Someone knew this truth two hundred years before I did:

> *Our lives is ever on the way*
> *And Death is ever nigh.*
> *The moment when our lives begin*
> *We all begin to die.*
> —a grave marker near Barrington, Vermont, 1792

Most of us prepare for birthing, schooling, graduating, marrying, getting and keeping a job, baptizing and confirming, but not for dying nor grieving. Yet in the midst of our living, we can all prepare to die.

I heard those words "She doesn't know" several years ago. Since then I've been asked many, many times, "Why are you still alive?" "What was your secret?" "Was it your experimental treatment?" "Was it a result of your laying-on-of-hands service?" "Was the secret medical, or was it spiritual?"

I don't know the answer. But I do know that my freedom to go on to live, and to live well, includes having *worked through my dying*.

From my own experience, I can assure you that it is liberating to make your choices and take care of the details. It has freed me from the ongoing, nagging worries that come from avoiding and procrastinating.

I now have the emotional and mental energy to accommodate new and life-fulfilling dreams: traveling to places I've always wanted to go, establishing a not-for-profit organization, and spending quality time with my family and dear friends. In other words, finding the *joy that life offers*. I can't say that I don't have my bad or weak or uncertain moments. But having resolved the thornier issues surrounding my death has freed me in a way I never thought possible.

And we must remember, our death is not ours alone. Our death affects many others.

We can and should prepare for our deaths out of a love for our loved ones! Preparing for our death is a gift, for better grief, for those who remain behind. Wise people tell us that we give what we want to receive; we teach what we want to learn. Here I'm writing what I wanted to read.

This book is about feelings and faith. It is not a how-to book. It is a "how-I-did-it" book; it is the story of one woman confronting her own death.

It's the story of a woman who can now live *joyfully*, knowing that, because she is ready to die, she doesn't have to be afraid to live. It is a testimonial that, even though we face death, we can still live—not only live, but live fully! As William Penn reflected much more eloquently, "We cannot love to live if we cannot bear to die."

Welcome to *Ready to Live, Prepared to Die!* It is personal and practical; part story and part checklist; my stories and my friends' stories; my struggles and theirs. It's also about the steps I've taken, decisions I've made, books I've read, and films I've watched.

A Different Kind of Journey I've loved to travel as long as I can remember. My friends have nicknamed me St. Amy of the Maps. I remember as a young girl, when traveling with my parents, I'd delve into the road maps and announce where we were, where we had been, and all the possibilities of how we could get where we wanted to go. Since those back-seat days, I've been in the front seat to all fifty states in the U.S. and to over sixty countries around the world.

It isn't surprising, then, that I've used the journey metaphor as a comfortable tool for planning my dying and death. I've structured this book around the several stages of planning and preparing for a trip.

I'm sharing the issues, options, and decisions I faced while preparing to die—so that you can consider and apply them to your situation. As you read, record your reactions right in the book! Write in the margins. Date and initial them. There is a more structured checklist in the back of the book, should you prefer to use it. Although this isn't a legal document and you can always change your mind, these notations will give you a good start for necessary communication. As you go forward, as you doubt, question, reflect, sort, and come to answers that are right for you, you have my warmest support.

I hope that revealing my own decisions and indecisions, and the experiences of others who have helped me, will help you prepare to die—so you can truly begin to *live the precious life you have!*

1

When My Journey Began

I'm an only child of upper-middle-class parents, who gave me a generous and loving environment to grow up in. Until 1985, I was your typical single, never-married, no children, working woman labeled by some a "career gal." I lived in a luxury high-rise apartment overlooking Michigan Avenue, with a view of Lake Michigan, in downtown Chicago. My suitably impressive consulting office was just six blocks away. My walk to and from work afforded world-class window shopping along the Miracle Mile. I was making solid money and living more than comfortably—enough to indulge my passion for travel. It might have been described as a "cruise ship" life.

Then I became a cancer patient.

When all the testing was done, I asked my doctor, "What are my odds?" He told me that fewer than twenty in one hundred women were still alive five years after a similar diagnosis.

I had invasive cervical cancer, with multiple lymph node involvement—very serious. While lymph node involvement is not of itself terminal, I had bilateral involvement, which was double jeopardy.

I Want to Live! It took my confrontation with cancer for me to ask the tough question: What did I want? The answer was very simple—I wanted to live!

So I signed up for an experimental protocol. My treatment required a week in the hospital followed by a week at home for R & R—which for me reflected retch and runs. This cycle was repeated six times. During five months I had four trips to the operating room, fifty radiation treatments, and thirty days of twenty-four-hour intravenous chemotherapy. To complete the experiment, I had a radiation implant requiring isolation. The treatment was called "the hammer," because it hit the cancer from both sides.

The tumor disappeared. But I was a very, very long shot for total cure.

Those five months were very difficult. However, I was supported and uplifted with calls, cards, visits, and prayers from friends and family near and far. I was particularly uplifted by many members from a church where I had worshiped prior to living in downtown Chicago. Wanting to thank the members from St. Mark's Episcopal Church in Geneva, Illinois, I asked Father Rick Lobs, my friend and priest, how I could thank the church community.

He invited me to share my gratitude at an adult Sunday school session. The room was packed. Afterwards, one of the ladies whom I didn't recognize came up to me and asked, "Is this story in print?" It turned out to be a woman whose husband had died of cancer that year. She was Luci Shaw, a nationally known poet and publisher, and she wanted to publish my talk. This resulted in my first book, *When Your Friend Gets Cancer*.

After writing the book, I seized opportunities to talk to and encourage people in person and through radio and TV. Several years later I was featured on "Living Well," hosted by Dr. Art Ulene. The TV crew filmed a radiologist who was reviewing C.T. scans of tumors. When he commented on my original tumor, not knowing who it belonged to, he said, "This person probably didn't make it." I spoke up and said, "That's me!" He and everyone else in the room burst into broad smiles. Thank God for experimental protocols!

I resumed my international consulting business and continued my old habits of traveling extensively. But work didn't hold the significance it once had. I found far more meaning and purpose in persuading people to approach, not avoid, their loved ones who have cancer. I encouraged men and women to reach out, offering helping hands and healing hearts.

I spoke wherever I could. With my negative prognosis, I saw no reason to have a retirement account. I used every dollar I had. I went many places all over the country, from Florida to Oregon, and addressed over one hundred audiences.

My cancer, however, had been spreading along the predicted path. In 1987, I had a metastatic recurrence to my right lung. I made two more trips to the operating room and had most of the lung removed.

My "B.I.D."— Before I Die

Have you ever been asked, "What would you like to do if you knew your life was going to end next year?" People often pose that question during the wee hours with a group of close friends. Sometimes it's thrown out as a challenge in a counseling session.

Many of us have our answers, but we postpone our actions. We wait until our twenty-fifth wedding anniversary, or until we're fifty-five years old—or sixty-two, or sixty-five.

With my newly discovered sense of aliveness, I thought I should answer the question right then: What *did* I want to do? After all, there might not be a later! It was time for me to do my B.I.D.—my "Before I Die." I had an incredible desire to take hold of life, to use it fully. It didn't take long for me to identify what I wanted to do.

Within months, I went to the bank and borrowed four thousand dollars. I had borrowed lumps of money over the years for cars, computers, and the like. The banker, accustomed to my coming to the loan desk, asked, with head lowered, eyes upon the loan paper and pen in hand, "What is the purpose of this loan?" I replied, "To swim with the sea lions."

Once upon a time I was a swimmer at the Elmhurst YMCA. As an eight- to twelve-year-old girl, I was very good at the backstroke. At ten years old, I was the fastest girl swimming the backstroke in the state of Illinois. Most days, my routine included swimming laps for ninety minutes. I loved to swim.

As many parents do, mine made the sacrifice of hauling me to the Y after school for swim team practices and to the Saturday meets. In the team practices we would swim over 75 laps, and then we would have ten minutes of play time.

My true joy was the exhilarating sensation of freedom, of the water rushing by my skin. I would head straight to the deep end, jump up and take a deep breath, and then let my weight sink me to the bottom in the deepest place. I'd bend my knees as my feet touched the bottom and then push up hard. It was marvelous, just getting to the bottom and then that joy of exploding upward. What fun to sink down . . . stay there quietly . . . and then *push up!* Down, and then *up*. Down, and then *up*.

My B.I.D. was to experience those childlike feelings again. I wanted to be in nature's pool with the best of the swimmers—the sea lions. And Nicholas, a client and friend of mine, told me that the best place in the world to swim with the sea lions was in the Galapagos Islands. I went there directly.

The Galapagos Islands look exactly like my image of Genesis 1:1. They are on the equator, off the west coast of Ecuador in the Pacific Ocean. Although a part of Ecuador, the islands, made famous by Charles Darwin, are an international wildlife refuge. They are named after the large box-shaped Galapagos tortoises that are found there.

The islands literally are the tops of volcanoes, ruggedly beautiful and abundant with wildlife: red and green iguanas; male frigates, who inflate their big red pouches in their necks when they're "in the mood"; penguins and pelicans. It's also the land of the famous blue-footed boobies. They really do have blue feet! There are hundreds of bird colonies.

But I went to the Galapagos to be with the sea lions—to swim with the sea lions—to experience that freedom and exhilaration I had as a child in the company of wild, free, graceful swimmers.

I shared a whirlwind swim with two sea lions in the middle of the Pacific Ocean. For three hours, I had my B.I.D.

Can you imagine me out there? I *played!* I went under the water and waited. A sea lion came and buzzed me and then suddenly swerved right over my shoulder. And then his playmate joined us. For three hours, I was in this threesome. We circled and somersaulted. We moved together in a synchronized water ballet. Never touching, we turned and twirled. They *played* with me! After a while, one sea lion moved on, but the other remained. I named him Sweet William. And we continued to swim until the sun set.

Every time I came up for air it was *God, take me now. I've had my B.I.D.; I'm ready.*

Well, God didn't take me. But I took memories of Sweet William with me, memories I'll have forever.

But the most important memory I have is what I learned with Sweet William. With William I learned to *play*. With William I learned to fulfill my life wish, to treat myself.

Fellow traveler, what is your "Before I Die" wish?

Treating myself to a life wish, to my B.I.D., was energizing. Then I could look at my life . . . and my death . . . and my living . . . and my dying . . . and begin to make the difficult choices that only I could make.

2

Pick Your Destination

You know the old saying "If you don't know where you're going, any road will take you there"? When I began preparing for my own death, I found I couldn't plan without knowing my destination. Where would I be after the moment of death? Where was I going? It helps to dream of our destination.

Consider the Possibilities

There was no question of my destination: heaven, of course! Mine was an automatic response because of an early childhood memory. Every night before I went to sleep, my mother would come into my room and we would pray together:

> *Now I lay me down to sleep,*
> *I pray the Lord my soul to keep.*
> *If I should die before I wake,*
> *I pray the Lord my soul to take.*

God bless Mommy, God bless Daddy,
God bless Grampy,
God bless Moe-Moe, and God bless Sam
    (our dogs).

Most of my friends have childhood memories of bedtime prayers. Yet I'm discovering many men and women haven't had such a fortunate past.

My vision of my afterlife was shaped as a camper at Honey Rock Camp, a camp run by Wheaton College, a well-known Christian liberal arts school. There I was assured that, having "accepted Jesus" (as a ten-year-old), I was guaranteed heaven forever.

Other possibilities didn't exist for me. I spent my entire life in the Protestant tradition and was never exposed to the concept of purgatory until I was in my thirties. The subject of hell received minimal comment in my circles as well. Heaven just seemed to be the obvious destination for me.

Although I assumed I wanted to go to heaven, I later spent a significant amount of time reviewing that choice. I wanted to know what I actually believed about heaven. I wanted to find out if the theology I was taught about heaven still rang as true in the heart of this adult person as it did in the child I had been.

Try as I might to find out about Heaven, the more frustrated I became. Thick-headed, I tried harder. Although the Bible offers some descriptions, I found them inadequate for my needs. They were told in apparent metaphors and fanciful descriptions. Perhaps they are literal, and I am too stubborn to accept their dimensions.

I love hearing other cultures and other religions depict the afterlife. But I found my comeuppance when reading some quotes from Jim Boulden's book, *Life and Death: A Collected Wisdom.* After reading these quotes and others like them, I finally chuckled at my need for certainty and resumed my childlike faith, reflected by descriptions such as these:

> *Heaven is a nice place to go, but nobody is in a rush to get there.*—Diane, age 10

> *When you die, you don't have to do homework in Heaven . . . unless your teacher is there too.*
> —Marsha, age 9

> *Only the good people go to Heaven, the other people go where it's hot all the time . . . like in Florida.*
> —Judy, age 9

Read the Guidebooks

After we dream of our typical trip or vacation, we often talk to others who have been there. We read books and magazines, listen to others' travel stories, and look at pictures. After I became convinced of my ultimate destination, I did what I always do. I went to the "travel planning" section of the community library and local bookstores and took out some books—in this case, on dying and the afterlife.

There weren't many books, but there were a few. I found the writings of Elizabeth Kubler-Ross, which I had studied twenty years before, while getting my master's degree in social service administration. I also spent considerable time reading and enjoying the works of Steve Levine. These books were comforting, but not satisfying. One book authored by a Christian meant a lot to me. It was the book *Facing Death* by Billy Graham. I found it both comforting and satisfying.

The more I read, the more I wanted to read. Many of these books are listed in the Bibliography.

In addition to reading books, I attended seminars. I traveled to Washington, D.C., to learn from Steve Levine; I went to Minneapolis to be with Ram Dass. I read a considerable amount of the NDE (near death experiences) literature.

It's interesting that I found more sources in the "reincarnation" sections of bookstores than in the "resurrection" sections. With this striking display of books before me, I started to reevaluate my earlier "of course" response for heaven. Was there really a heaven?

I was embarrassed by my skepticism and lack of certainty. As a result, I went off to travel the temples from Bali to Borneo. I wanted to see the places of worship, to dialogue with the worshipers, and to compare my own beliefs to theirs. I have talked with men and women of the Jewish, Muslim, Hindu, Sufi, and Buddhist traditions.

When I returned, I started to listen seriously to what was being said in my church's service. I asked myself, "Do I understand what I'm saying here; do I *believe* what I'm saying here?" I labored over the difference between the Nicene Creed and the Apostles' Creed. It mattered to me that one recorded that Jesus descended to hell and the other didn't. I wanted to know why.

Debate the Decision Through all my reading and thinking, I realized that understanding our destination shapes all we do in preparing for the trip, and it especially determines our enthusiasm to take the trip.

I minored in religions of the world in college. I have traveled to sixty countries on six continents. I remain fascinated by the variety of practices of worshiping God the Creator. I remember being in Kuala Lumpur, Malaysia, and strolling through a modern market place. I found an English book store, and in it I found a section on religion. What a small world; I found a book published fifteen miles from my hometown on the other side of the world called *Religions*, published by David C. Cook. In that book, as in many others of that type, faith traditions divide over a very significant issue: Does the person believe in reincarnation, or does he or she believe in the possibility for resurrection?

After considerable internal questioning and anguish, I knew I had to make up my mind. Although I had started my quest for detailed knowledge to help me plan for my dying, a by-product was a crisis; I needed to decide whether or not to join the people in my church in saying aloud the words to our creeds.

When I dared to ask questions, I felt summarily dismissed with instructions to go read the Scriptures. But the more I read, the more confused I became. I read authors and educators for answers to my questions, and found that they had different conclusions.

The thought of reincarnation became appealing because of its simplicity in denying both heaven and hell. There is a very appealing and slippery temptation for people like me, who struggle with some sermons and Scriptures, to select another path that seems less difficult.

I tried very hard using my thinking to pick my destination, and my thoughts failed me. When I switched tactics and returned to my childhood practices, I became far more successful.

The Christian tradition proclaims the words of Jesus to be true: "I am the way." I thank God that I was brought up by parents who brought their daughter to church and escorted her into Sunday school class. I have chosen Christ. It is a most personal decision, and the reasons are not simple, but I explain them briefly here.

First, I know I can never be good enough or perfect enough to earn a desirable afterlife. I would rather rely on that mysterious grace of Jesus and his gift of life than have to try so hard at something I cannot accomplish for myself. This is the Christian concept of *grace*. Grace involves acceptance by God and existence with God even after our physical bodies are gone.

Second, as a seasoned traveler, my habits are ingrained. I am a traveler who travels *to* someplace, not *from* someplace. Most devotees of reincarnation travel from someplace, preferring to spin from negativity to a place without negativity. I choose heaven with a vision of it as a real place to go, not as an empty space.

And finally, I've lived my life fully appreciating relationships. For most of my adult years, my primary relationship has been with God. I want to continue my most prized relationship. I choose resurrection to be with God.

I heard a young girl comment with her environmentally conscious language that she would "prefer to piggyback on Jesus than to go and recycle dozens and dozens of times to get to Heaven." I'm sure her theology would be corrected by scholars, but I think her insight is worthy to be heard.

As a child on frequent car trips with my parents, in the back seat with my maps, I had full confidence, relying on my childlike faith that we would get to our destination. Now, with another trip in mind and using that same childlike faith, "I pick heaven, of course!"

If I should die before I wake,
I pray the Lord my soul to take.

Pack Your Care Package

On my most recent car trip, I drove forty-two hundred miles. I had a hefty bag full of sand in the trunk in case I got stuck in the snow, a blanket in the back seat for sub-zero cold, a half-gallon of windshield de-icer, and candles in a tin. In addition to these contingencies for my car, I had supplies for me, too: bakery goods, bottles of water, and plenty of coffee. I have learned to pack a care package. And I have loving friends who ensure that I take what I need.

Although I don't have bags of sand and blankets and snacks for tackling my preparing-to-die tasks, I have supplied myself with a personally crafted care package for this difficult journey toward death. I rely on Scripture, song, and symbols to see me safely to heaven, my destination.

Scripture. I rely on the standards: the Lord's Prayer, the Twenty-third Psalm, Psalm 121, John 3:16. They have deep meaning for me. I have two favorites for my most critical times: John 3:17, "For God did not send his Son into the world to be its judge, but to be its Savior," and verses recited during Communion, especially Matthew 11:28, "Come to me, all you who are weary and burdened, and I will give you rest." I replenish my care package reading my morning devotions in *Forward Day by Day*.

Song. Periodically, on this difficult journey, I tap into my song package. To energize, renew, and kick myself out of the blues, I play songs by the country artist K.T. Oslin. At other times I find myself recalling those songs from my childhood that are akin to "comfort food" when you're down. They rekindle my childlike faith. Whenever I feel inept or frustrated, I find myself humming, "Jesus loves me, this I know, for the Bible tells me so," and "What a friend we have in Jesus, all our sins and griefs to bear." And, finally, when I really need to soar into being or feeling (rather than doing or thinking), I put on one of two CDs: *Spirituals in Concert* with Kathleen Battle and Jessye Norman, or *Ave Maria* with Kiri Te Kanawa. And recently I've begun to develop a penchant for classical oboe music.

Symbols. Some of us are visual; some of us are auditory; and some of us are kinetic, I'm told. People come in all types, and I know what I am. I am visual. If I had a large family, I would be mentioning people in this section. My eyes might see my husband and children, and I imagine that I would be sustained by their smiles and eyes.

But I'm the only one who lives in my home. And while it started haphazardly, it is now intentional that within my eyesight, whichever chair I sit in, I can always see three symbols. There is either a sculpture, painting, wall hanging, or ornament of a sea lion or otter, an angel, and a lamb. While tackling some of my very tough tasks, I absorb the meaning and significance from my icons or symbols with just a glance in their direction.

While I know of their challenges of survival, sea otters symbolize for me a spirit of playfulness and glee. They always strike me as happy. They have a can-do attitude. They are independent.

The Bible says angels are messengers. Whenever I see an angel, the message I receive is "You are not alone."

Not surprisingly, when I see a lamb or a sheep, I am always reminded that the Lord is my Shepherd.

Tackle the To-Dos

Society has sanitized death. In general, we have a reluctance to confront our mortality. For many of us, the thought of preparing for our death is difficult. Yet planning for our death in an orderly fashion can give us peace. It is also a loving and beautiful gift for our loved ones, who will experience grief and loss when we are gone. We have an obligation to "get our house in order."

Do you have your house in order? There are different points of view on what that means. To doctors, it might mean signed organ donor cards, a living will, a durable power of attorney for health care on file. For financial planners, it might mean having your money in stocks or bonds or in a trust. People in my church have said their house was in order, because they are ready from a religious or spiritual point of view. A lawyer at my golf club has said, "I'm ready—my will is up-to-date." Unfortunately, these are narrowly focused and, as a result, are incomplete. The metaphor of a house in order originally referred to the complete scope of details that need to be addressed.

Recently I worked with a group of family doctors. I asked them, "If you received a diagnosis from one of your colleagues that you were seriously ill, what would you do to get your house in order?" I was pleased by the diversity and detail of their responses.

Imagine you were going to take a cruise. You would hope for smooth sailing but would expect some rough waters occasionally. Consequently, you would probably pack sea-sickness pills. You would have a list of errands to run, which might include getting cash and travelers' checks, picking up cleaning, prepaying some bills, going to the shoe repair, taking your animals to the kennel, writing instructions to leave lights on or off for security, and having the post office hold your mail.

I approached preparing to die by making a similar list of to-dos. This book lists the questions I have asked myself, and some of my personal choices and conclusions. The goal is to motivate you to do whatever you can, and to encourage you to remember two things:

- The to-do list is doable!
- It's not sufficient for you to consider only what *you* want or don't want. Your death also belongs to your loved ones. You must think of what they want as well, because they will carry the consequences of your choices and decisions forever.

In preparing for your own dying and death, I strongly encourage you to apply these guidelines to each of the difficult topics that follow:

1. *Examine your values,* which will shape your options. For example, does your religious denomination require, suggest, or dictate a full body burial?

2. *Identify your options.* Brainstorm and think creatively. For example, how do you want to personalize your funeral or memorial service?

3. *Communicate your choices* to your loved ones, face to face. For example, who is your pre- ferred guardian for your children? What are your instructions for organ donation?

4. *Document your decisions,* fully complying with specific state laws. Be sure to distribute copies of your decisions to your significant others and professionals. For example, does your primary health care professional have a copy of your durable power of attorney for health care?

Choosing the logical sequence for these to-dos has been difficult. I recognize that everyone has his or her own way to get ready for a trip. And each of us has our own way to organize our closet, our desk, and our briefcase. In each of these situations, there is no right or wrong way. Likewise, there's no right way to plan for our dying.

While I have organized these difficult topics into logical groupings, I did not experience them in this order. I did, however, try to arrange the issues so that anyone—the healthy and the not-so-healthy—can proceed with this sequence.

We will start with the most practical issues, pro- ceed through more personal issues, and conclude with those most spiritual. They are clustered so that you might choose to seek professional guidance more eas- ily. For some questions you might seek medical ad- vice. For others you might seek the counsel of a lawyer. For others you might speak with a counselor or a social worker. And for the remaining, a spiritual adviser or member of the clergy might be helpful. These professionals could be thought of as your travel consultants.

In the end of the book, there is a checklist, with room for you to record your thoughts, desires, and decisions regarding the issues that are discussed in the following chapters. Feel free to jot down, throughout the book, anything you want to remember to do or communicate at a later time.

You will also find listed some books and films I have found helpful.

3

Heroic Efforts and the Suicide Question

I've had ten operations. And to have the quality of life that I now have, I'd gladly have ten more. But I know there will be a time when I won't want another operation or another procedure. Some might think at that time that I will be giving up. However, I think I will say to those men and women that my behavior will not reflect giving up, but moving on.

I've started with this topic because I think there will likely be a time when many of us will think of medical technology as an interference with, not a help to, our dying.

Those of us who want to live as long as we can should have no fear. Our medical technology is able to help prolong life. Doctors take the Hippocratic Oath, vowing to sustain life.

During the 1980s and 1990s high tech has pushed our limits, medically and ethically. Professionals and the public are spending a tremendous amount of time, money, and energy discussing how we, as a society, can blend the traditions of health and ethics and faith and resolve difficult situations, including genetic engineering, surrogate motherhood, bionic parts, and end-of-life decisions.

Part of the blessing of sudden death is not having to work through all the choices that confront one whose death is more prolonged. Those dying of a lingering illness often reach a point where they don't want to be "maintained."

Andrew Malcolm, in his autobiography, *Someday, the Story of a Mother and Her Son,* reported, "The American Hospital Association estimates that 70 percent of the six thousand deaths that occur in the United States every day are somehow negotiated and timed."

Understanding this dramatic statement requires us to think about which heroic efforts we would want, or not want. Under what conditions would we want our deaths to be "negotiated and timed"?

Throughout the United States, health care providers and institutions have implemented a policy called "informed consent." We are accountable for our own health care and have this legal protection to make our own choices with the Patient Self Determination Act.

In 1990, the American Medical Association published a form, The Medical Directive. The AMA listed medical interventions ranging from pain medication to resuscitation. These interventions are considered by some to be heroic and by others to be routine. We should think about and decide which ones we would want or not want used in our dying days. Some of us might welcome some of these interventions; others would be distraught if they were applied. The list includes:

- cardiopulmonary resuscitation
- mechanical breathing

- artificial nutrition and hydration
- major surgery
- kidney dialysis
- chemotherapy
- minor surgery
- invasive diagnostic tests
- blood or blood products
- antibiotics
- simple diagnostic tests
- pain medication

We must confront our values and beliefs to determine what is right for us. In addition, we might think of what our tradition holds dear. Jewish, Christian, Islamic, Hindu, and Buddhist religions each have definite views of life and death. Whatever your spiritual background—including agnosticism and atheism—your view of living and dying has been shaped by that background. You may disagree with traditional beliefs, but it is still important for you to look at them carefully. Your choices regarding your dying should be *conscious*, not automatic.

When we consider heroic efforts, in addition to reviewing this range of interventions, we must also think of the circumstances surrounding us. The situations include:

- a terminal illness
- a chronic debilitating disease
- a permanent disability
- an irreversible coma or persistent vegetative state
- a coma with a very slight chance of recovery
- irreversible brain damage with a terminal illness
- irreversible brain damage without a terminal illness

There are many options and many variables. For example, if I am in a car wreck, would I want heroic efforts to save my life? *(Yes! Save me!)* Since I have lost most of one lung, if my remaining lung were to become cancerous, would I want to be on a respirator until it heals? *(Yes)* If my heart should fail, should I be resuscitated? *(Only if I will be assured of . . . what?)* Nor can we presume to know what another would want. I told my friend Gordon that I didn't want shocks if my heart were to stop. He, however, had a history of heart disease, and he told me that the paddles are a friend to him—that they give his heart a needed "jump start"—and are, of course, desired by him.

Joni Earickson Tada shares her conclusions in her recent book *When Is It Right To Die? Suicide, Euthanasia, Suffering, Mercy*, emphasizing what is *not* appropriate for her. Deciding what we don't want is also making a positive step.

If heroic measures will provide me quality time, then I want doctors to do what can be done. If there will be no significant quality or quantity of time to be gained by heroic measures, then I want them withheld. My belief that heaven is a desirable place to be means, for me, that there is no need to extend my stay here on earth through heroic efforts, since I'm on a journey to everlasting life.

During my process of determining what was right for me, I saw a documentary film, *Near Death*, that was a turning point. The film featured live documentary footage of four families in the intensive care unit at Beth Israel Hospital in Boston. At the end of each patient's life, it was hard for the patients to articulate their desires and to make thoughtful decisions. Their families struggled to agree what should have been done, adding more stress to already stressful situations.

It became clear to me, through watching this film, that heroic efforts are not an independent decision. They become a family decision. And if it matters for you to have your wishes carried out, then you need to tell people *in advance* what you want—and put your wishes in writing. Don't wait till the end, or you may discover that you won't get what you want.

Suicide—Assisted and Otherwise

When people use suicide as their means to continue their spiritual journey into the afterlife, "self-deliverance" is the phrase frequently used. Unfortunately, there are many examples of attempts that have failed, when the individual didn't die. Sadly, the individual often becomes more debilitated. As a result, patients are now seeking assistance from their health care providers, friends, and family members to assure death. This collaboration is now referred to as "assisted suicide" or "active euthanasia." In the past, this behavior was referred to as "mercy killing."

It's practically impossible these days to pick up a newspaper anywhere in the country without seeing an article on Dr. Jack Kevorkian or assisted suicide. In the *Chicago Tribune*, there have been over twenty-five articles in the past year alone. Assisted suicide, and the issues surrounding it, have become one of the hottest topics on our national agenda.

After I received my negative prognosis, I became more and more sensitive to the subject of suicide. I read Betty Rollins's book *Last Wish*, where she shares her true story of helping her mother die. I've also read the books of Derek Humphrey, *Let Me Die Before I Wake*, and the bestseller *Final Exit*. In addition, I've followed the work of the Hemlock Society, and I've tracked various state legislatures' debates. I subscribe to *Second Opinion* and *The Hastings Report*.

This subject is still taboo to many people of religious faith, Christian and otherwise. *But we cannot close our eyes to the many patients each year who turn to suicide as a means of maintaining some control over their dying.* In many cases, the patient cannot bear the thought of long-term, excruciating pain. In others, the person has lost his or her sense of purpose or usefulness. Some people take their lives in order to spare friends and family members the lengthy and exhausting process of caring for them. They often fear becoming a burden and leaving daunting medical expenses after months of intensive or specialized care. Undoubtedly, some of these people would not choose suicide if they were assured proper pain management or were helped to see the value of their lives. Yet, some people, after thinking carefully, would still choose active euthanasia.

Regardless of the beliefs you may have held all your life, when faced with terminal illness and all it involves, you may discover yourself considering active euthanasia, or assisted suicide, as an option. We cannot ignore the gut-level, honest questions that enter our hearts and minds during times of crisis and pain. This is not the time to be ashamed and silent about what we are considering. Neither is it a time to stop talking to loved ones about our spiritual struggles and our choices. Rather, it is a time for much prayer, meditation, communication, and clear thinking. Take time—to think and meditate on your own beliefs, to talk with your friends and family, to read and reflect upon Scripture and other literature that is meaningful to you. Clarify your own thinking, and then look at your living options. Hospice organizations can help you identify these options.

I have great empathy for those men and women who want to exercise more control over their dying and death. I respect hospice care, and a major tenet of hospice care is that aggressive pain management usually alleviates the felt need for taking one's own life.

Faced with the final weeks and months of my life, I don't know what my decisions will be. But I hope and pray that I will have the grace to defer the timing of my death to God, believing that the Lord's Prayer is the best recommendation for our living and our dying: "Thy will be done."

Questions to consider

(For more space to record your thoughts, see the Ready to Live Checklist on page 141.)

What heroic efforts do I want?
> (e.g., none, cardiac resuscitation, respiratory support, artificial sustenance and hydration)

Under what conditions do I wish heroic efforts withheld or withdrawn?
> (e.g., coma, persistent vegetative state)

Are there preparatory actions I should take?

What are my feelings about "self-deliverance" and "assisted suicide"?

Have I talked with loved ones about my feelings and wishes concerning heroic efforts and self-deliverance?

4

Advance
Directives

Most of us remain competent until our final moment
of death. Not only are we able to participate in our care;
we manage our care. We stay in charge with our
"informed consent." However, many of us will not
remain competent until the end. Unfortunately, some
interventions that are intended to keep us alive often
cloud our thinking. Losing control is one of the strong-
est fears that most of us have.

When we are no longer able to supervise and
implement our wishes, our families and health care
providers are usually able to reach an acceptable con-
sensus as to what to do.

But numerous newspaper headlines and national
stories have recently captured our attention. These
stories revolve around the ethical and legal questions
"Whose body is it? Whose decision is it?" At stake here
are issues of responsibility and accountability, wrapped

around the hot topic of heroic efforts. The more I heard of the cases of Karen Ann Quinlan, Nancy Cruzan, Elizabeth Bouvia, and Christine Busalacchi, the more anxious I became.

Now I know why we must rely on formal and legally accepted documents. We must delegate to others the permission and power to implement our wishes on our behalf if we are no longer able to do so. *Advance directives* is the generic term for these instructions: specific documents include: the living will, the durable power of attorney for health care, and the durable power of attorney for property. These become most useful "in case of emergency."

Living Will Today when you are admitted to a hospital, some of the first questions you are asked are, "Do you have a living will?" followed by "Do you have a durable power of attorney for health care?"

The purpose of a living will is to communicate to the doctor and/or the hospital certain key points. The patient can express with this document that he or she does or does not want heroic efforts. However, living wills apply only if the patient is suffering from a life-threatening illness and if the health care professionals agree that death is likely to come soon.

When I was having my experimental protocol, the popular advance directive was the living will. I can remember when living will forms were available in drug stores. Signs were posted in shop windows, advertising that they were available for sale. However, then and now, living wills vary from state to state and from hospital to hospital. There is no national, standardized legal format.

Living wills are especially helpful in blended and extended families, where there may be differences of opinion as to who knows best what the patient would want.

In the 1990s, the living will is still useful for showing a patient's intent, but it has significant limitations. For example, in most cases it does not apply for men and women who are in a PVS (permanent vegetative state) resulting from a car accident. Moreover, living wills have often been challenged successfully by family members, who say that the author of the living will did not know what they were doing when they signed the document. Living wills are also contested by special interest groups. These nonrelatives often successfully petition the court to hold or stop the enactment of a patient's living will, using right-to-life arguments.

I have signed and distributed copies of my living will.

Durable Power of Attorney for Health Care

As I've said, the living will applies to certain situations only. Because of its limited scope, many people are now delegating health care decisions to one person with the durable power of attorney for health care (DPA/HC). The DPA/HC is a legal document that names an agent to make health care decisions on behalf of the person who is unable to express wishes for himself or herself.

Although this instrument does not specifically articulate the various procedures and protocols you would like, it does provide you a place to list specific preferences and restrictions for your care. Although you are giving complete control to another human being, you can limit, by law, what that person can do on your behalf.

When discussing heroic efforts, it can become very difficult to consider what you would like to have done or not done, since there are so many possible scenarios you might face. Therefore, most people delegate full authority to their agent and trust what the agent will judge appropriate. Whatever your agent dictates must be upheld by your physicians and the hospital. The court must also support your agent.

The durable power of attorney for health care is much more powerful than the living will. Also, the durable power of attorney for health care provides a means for delegating authority to a non-relative, an important consideration for single adults.

Choosing your agent
When you prepare a durable power of attorney for health care, you are empowering another person to make your decisions. In essence, you are giving them full authority to listen to or ignore the advice of your doctor or institution. Therefore, it is critical that you share your values and discuss your wishes with this person.

Choosing a person who will have the authority to act on your behalf is not easy. Yet we must think ahead. To whom will we delegate decision-making authority? Who will have the duty to make difficult choices and, if necessary, "pull the plug"?

For whomever you choose as your agent, it will be a difficult role to fulfill. Your agent will be held accountable by their own conscience and by the opinion of every person who has had an interest in your living and dying.

Therefore, *discuss your wishes for heroic efforts with all those who care about you.* If you don't share your values with everyone, you increase the likelihood for bitter feuds over your care and lasting family strife. In addition, these discussions will help minimize possible objections to your agent's actions on your behalf.

The selection process and criteria for an agent vary widely. It really depends on your current situation and family dynamics. When I've asked others who they've chosen, they replied:

"My oldest child—because he's the oldest."

"The child living closest to home because she's closer to us and the hospital."

"My husband." (Or, "*Not* my husband!")

Remember, it is not essential for the person holding your durable power of attorney for health care to be a blood relative or spouse! Some people pick a close friend "who knows me best"—someone they have trusted with confidences. Others prefer to relieve their loved ones of the decision and ask an objective party, a lawyer for example, who might have more experience acting as an agent.

You can only appoint *one* person. You cannot make a joint appointment. Of course your agent can ask the opinions of others, but ultimately, only that one person's signature will go on documents executed on your behalf. The DPA/HC form provides for an alternate agent who will be called if the first person is unwilling or unable to continue to serve; for example, if he or she is on active military duty or out of the country.

Actually, you have a triple challenge. The first is to find the right person. Then you must obtain the acceptance of that person to act as your agent. There are times when the person you would choose might not be willing to take the responsibility. For example, a parent might pick the adult child they feel closest to emotionally, without realizing that their wishes conflict with that child's religious beliefs.

Finally, having chosen your agent, consider sharing with your family members the reasoning you used in choosing your agent and alternate. Help everyone to understand your thinking so that they will be better able to respect the difficult decisions your agent must make.

A difficult conversation

I've had a living will for a long time. But I soon realized how important it was to have a DPA/HC. It became apparent that I needed to appoint an agent. I called my parents to ask if I might come for a visit to discuss my DPA/HC. I flew down to the Carolina mountains, making this a specific event.

My parents and I have never found it easy to talk about death and dying. I told them I needed to complete this document because I led retreats that dealt with this issue, and I felt like a fraud for not having appointed my agent for durable power of attorney, as I was instructing others to do. This rationale gave us an opening to talk.

It was far easier for all of us to have this discussion in the context of helping me as a speaker and retreat leader. This agenda was different from staring boldly at my impending death. We were giving me credentials, helping me as an "expert" to practice what I preached. By approaching the conversation in this way, we were less tense, the conversation was less death oriented, and we were all less emotional.

Still, despite the technique that started us talking, the issue was still there: Who was I going to ask to perform this duty? I didn't know.

I remember crisp, clean air as I sat out on the screened porch, facing my mother and father. There was no table between us, and we were close together. I leaned in toward them. We were like the three corners of a triangle. It was hard for me to discuss this issue because we all saw through my manipulation.

This type of conversation has to be one of the most intimate a person can ever have. Who did I want, and who didn't I want; who did I trust, and who didn't I trust?

As I remember, I said, "I've been thinking of who would be appropriate to be my agent. Recognizing that I am a single, middle-aged woman, I've thought about who would care most about my death. I finally decided that since you both created me and I come from you, it's reasonable for me to come to you first and ask one of you to be my agent, before I go and ask my friends. I couldn't live with myself if I asked my friends before asking you."

I just didn't want to give a friend the power to let their daughter die, or to end her life, without asking them first. A DPA/HC applies to everything—to accidents and non-life-threatening situations, as well. Even whether to withhold food and water.

I continued, "I've thought about feelings. Only one of you will be able to have the formal legal right. One of you must live with the other's decision. How would that person live with the other's choice? The spillover from that one decision might conceivably influence the rest of your lives.

"I don't even know what criteria to use to choose: The oldest? The wisest? The male? The female?"

I said to myself, *One of you could do this more coolly, more calculatedly, more clinically—and the other would do it with more of a spiritual bent and angle.*

"What do you think?" I asked. I don't know if I was acting like a chicken in my evasive, passive posturing, or if I was honestly consulting with them.

This thirty-minute conversation was one of the most difficult conversations I've ever had. Not because of the people involved, but because of the content.

Yet families who don't have this conversation before someone becomes sick must deal with serious repercussions later.

Although I was healthy and focused throughout this conversation, under the strain of the moment, I don't remember the sequence of sentences that followed. I only remember how uncomfortable I felt. And the outcome? The "older one" accepted the duty; and the "younger one" agreed to be the alternate. As situations change, relationships change, and health changes. Remember, you can always change your agent. It is better to appoint someone now than to not appoint anyone.

After you identify your agent and alternate, legal papers have to be executed. Although a living will can be executed on a form without a lawyer, with a durable power of attorney, it is critical to have a lawyer involved because of the powers of this instrument.

Whether or not you are facing a life-threatening illness, I encourage you to think seriously about preparing a living will and a durable power of attorney for health care, for the sake of your loved ones who will survive you. By making your intentions known, and by selecting a person to decide issues involving your care, you will make the stress of your last days easier for those you love.

Durable Power of Attorney for Property

Many people are familiar with a durable power of attorney for property. It's often considered proper and customary to delegate to another person the duty of managing one's assets and business affairs. These affairs include paying bills and shifting money between accounts. Bankers or capable family members are often selected to serve for people who don't want to deal with administrative details concerning assets. Many parents give such power to their adult children to act on their behalf. When we are unable to manage our affairs because of illness, hospitalization, or nursing home care, it is appropriate for an agent to have our durable power of attorney for property.

Appointing someone with this authority is an act of great trust. You want to be very sure of the person who will have direct access to your financial accounts.

While I have an executor for managing the details of my will, I do not yet have a durable power of attorney for property. By writing this section, I realize that I, too, have an outstanding "to-do."

Questions to consider

Do I want to sign a living will?

Is my living will signed and witnessed?

Who should have a copy of my living will in their possession?
> (e.g., lawyer, family members, certain friends, clergy)

Whom do I want to be involved in difficult health care decisions about my care and life support if I am incapable?
> (e.g., physician, lawyer, family member, friend)

Do I want to sign a durable power of attorney for health care (DPA/HC)?

Do my key family members understand and accept my choices for my designated primary and alternate agent(s)/attorney(s) for my DPA/HC?

Who should have a copy of my durable power of attorney for health care in their possession?
> (e.g., clergy, lawyer, friend, family member, physician)

Do I want to sign a durable power of attorney for property (DPA/P)?

Do my key family members understand and accept my choices for my designated primary and alternate agent(s)/attorney(s) for my DPA/P?

Who should have a copy of my durable power of attorney for property in their possession?

(e.g., clergy, lawyer, friend, family member, physician)

5

Instructions

Advance directives are one type of instructions. As we've discussed, they are delegated duties to be followed if we are no longer able to make decisions for ourselves.

However, there are several other important areas for us to consider and plan for appropriately. We can now move on and think about what will become of our favorite persons and possessions after we die.

Before we discuss what we would wish for our loved ones and our property, let's take a look at our thoughts about the disposition of our body.

Organ Donation

Pull out your driver's license. Turn it over and look at the back. Does your license have a designated *EXERCISE* space where you permit your body or parts to be used for organ transplants? Is your license signed? Is your signature witnessed?

Organ donation is not a subject that many people are comfortable discussing. However, you may be one who wants his or her body to have some value after your death.

There is a great need for organs; every day people die waiting for available ones. There are over thirty thousand men, women, and children waiting for these "gifts of life." It's quite possible that you know someone who could benefit from a transplant. Within one mile of my home, a teenage boy and a middle-aged father have recently benefited from donated organs.

If you want to give the gift of life, do it!

When I, having such widespread cancer involvement, considered the issue of organ donation, my first question was: What parts of my body still have value? Could I still give the gift of life to another person? I learned that because I am a cancer patient, I can donate neither blood nor organs, because it is still possible that cancer cells may remain throughout my body. Yet my corneas are usable! And my body can be used for research or experimentation.

I've heard several objections about organ donation. When I asked about the reasons for those objections, I heard people say that they wanted their loved ones intact for their wake and funeral services. I pursued this matter further. A funeral home director assured me that many people whose bodies are used for organ donation can still be prepared for a wake, and often in an open casket, within forty-eight hours.

Despite the great need, no medical institution will take organs unless the institutions are certain that it is the wish of the donor. They need immediate access to ensure a successful transplant. Therefore, take the following steps to give your gift of life.

Decide to do it. Anyone who decides to make an organ donation should do so legally. That means you must both sign your declaration of intent and have your signature witnessed in writing, presumably on the back of your driver's license or on an organ donor card. If you do not do this, no hospital will accept your donated organs, because it can't take the risk that some family member will disagree.

Share your decision with loved ones. For some, this second step is a harder one, but it is essential. Any objections or complaints by a significant other or a close relative can invalidate your legally witnessed consent. Hospitals simply do not want to confront your survivors and will honor their objections.

There can be unexpected reactions from people close to you. Some people may have a religious tradition that says the body must be whole for resurrection. If you hear objections based on religious principles, your local organ donation society can provide you with literature to help overcome the objections of your loved ones. With family members or loved ones, you may need to be bold. Have courage, and be committed to your decision.

Years ago I signed my driver's license to permit organ donation. Shortly after my original diagnosis, I received my new driver's license. When I realized that I had not had the new license witnessed, I dropped by my best friend's place of business to get her signature. I walked in and greeted her and her husband, pulled out my license very nonchalantly, and asked them to sign it. I said, "I need two witnesses; would you two witness for me?" I was surprised when she hesitated and flushed. I could feel her resistance and confusion. She looked at me thoughtfully and said, "Are you sure? Does it have to be now?" I had not anticipated such a reaction from someone so close to me. It was awkward. Yet, in the end, they lovingly signed after I insisted that it was my wish. Ironically, if I had asked two state employees at the driver's license bureau or my banker or a casual acquaintance to sign, they would have done it matter-of-factly and without hesitation. They would have had no emotional attachment. With my loved ones, signing the donor card was an acknowledgment of my mortality and not a gift of life, as I viewed it. I know that if I had asked the same question prior to my illness, they wouldn't have given it a second thought.

Realize that you may be putting your witnesses in an uncomfortable position. They may choose not to sign for you. And if they don't refuse outright, they might dodge by denying your need to do it. They might try to put witnessing off to some later date. If this happens, you might want to find another witness—someone who is less emotionally involved.

My driver's license recently expired again. I was thrilled to have lived long enough to retire the last one! This time when I went back to the same friends to ask for signatures, there were no problems or hesitations.

Guardianship

You will leave your possessions behind when you die, but perhaps you will also leave behind people, your children and your elders.

Minors. When we think of ourselves in the guardianship role, it is classically with children who are minors—underage children who need to be provided for. Typically, guardianship is given to a person who will provide personal care, food, shelter, etc. In addition, there might also be a trustee who will be in charge of the financial well-being of the child. Most often, these are the two separate people appointed when there are large sums of money involved.

To identify the appropriate legal guardian for your loved one, determine which characteristics are most appropriate. Should they be firm and loving; share your spiritual beliefs and values; live close to school, community, friends, or relatives? Should they be capable of developing the personality, hobbies, and talents of the child? To choose a guardian, select someone who shares your values—friends or family members—and who is compatible with the child.

A financial trustee is usually selected because of their ability to handle complex financial matters.

An important aspect of selecting a guardian is frequently overlooked: the compatibility of the guardian and the financial trustee. If the two are not compatible, there are certain to be disagreements along the way that could have an impact on the child; for example, about schooling choices, vacations, or allowances.

Be certain to ask your intended guardians if they are willing and able to accept the responsibility. It is unfair to those who will be asked to assume the responsibility to place your intentions in a sealed envelope, to be opened after your death. Potential guardians will wonder if they are, in fact, your choice. The guardianship role affects many conscious and unconscious decisions. For example, potential guardians might not feel free to relocate for a career change, feeling that they must remain close and available. When guardianship is decided and revealed ahead of time, the actual guardians can adjust their own plans—and others are freed from the anxiety.

Elders. People are living longer, and medicine has made great strides toward improving the life and well-being of our aging population. Financial or legal guardianship for our elders is a distinct possibility that we should consider and plan for. The process for appointing a guardian for an elder is just as complicated as that for a minor, perhaps even more so.

I witnessed a very touching event in the life of my friend Polly. Her mother had deteriorated significantly, and it became necessary for Polly to petition the court for her legal guardianship. I remember the sorrow, seeing the tears rolling down Polly's cheek, when she formalized this new legal role.

Since I am an only child, my parents have no immediate family, other than me, that they can rely on to be caregivers in their later years. Since we all assumed that they would outlive me following my diagnosis and prognosis, their solution has been to enter a lifetime care center.

While they are vital and strong and able to care for themselves, they are in a beautiful private townhome. If their needs for medical attention or supervision change, they will gradually move to different housing within the same community. There they will receive twenty-four-hour nursing access, and/or hospice care if needed. Now they are developing new friendships and are becoming part of their new community.

I am grateful for this loving gesture. They have planned their own retirement in such a way that they have ensured their care for the rest of their lives, even if I am not around to help.

Estate Planning

Local newspapers regularly carry articles on end-of-year tax and estate planning. There are many techniques for making tax-free investments and for leaving assets to loved ones prior to your death. If your estate is valued at $600,000 or more, or you have specific assets, you might speak with a financial planner to determine your options for retaining as much of your estate as is legally possible.

If you put your property into an estate, in addition to receiving tax savings, your beneficiaries will have quicker access to their inheritance. Having your assets in a trust can also give the added benefit of keeping your financial affairs private, not subject to public disclosure.

I've skipped this step in planning for my death because my assets haven't been significant enough to warrant it. Nor is it necessary to keep my affairs private.

Only one out of three people has a will. Yet everyone, even the homeless, has something. So why is it that the majority of people don't make a will? Some common reasons given are: **Wills**

- I don't have much money.
- I don't know how to make one or what's involved.
- I can't afford a lawyer.
- I don't care who gets what.
- Everyone already knows what I want them to have.

These responses are honest. However, most people don't recognize that these comments are inviting trouble and that, in some cases, they are simply wrong. When a person dies without a will (or "intestate"), our society has delegated the disposition of that person's goods to the legal system. When we die without a will, the courts determine how our assets will be distributed. The actual process varies from state to state, and it is most often a long and arduous one. At times the process is very costly to the beneficiaries. Sometimes a person's assets are frozen until the disposition of the case. This can take over two years!

Most states will honor a handwritten note signed by the departed. However, legal advice and proper legal form are preferable to ensure that your wishes are obeyed. Generally, we think of wills as documents that allow us to leave money or possessions; the will tells how they are to be distributed. I am personally struck by how often wills regard only money. It is quite acceptable and even desirable to put comments regarding special possessions into your will. For many people, possessions have greater sentimental value than a money inheritance. Specific instruction regarding how to distribute possessions is tremendously valuable because the directions prevent disagreements among survivors later.

Distributing your money and property. Wills are an effective mechanism for leaving stocks, bonds, cash, and property to those we choose. And we do have the right to delegate and bequeath our wealth, however small, the way we choose. I had a will prior to my diagnosis. What became critical afterwards was my willingness to update it. We often make a will and file it away, neither reviewing it regularly nor updating it periodically. Circumstances and relationships often change. Have you added a child to your family and not to your will?

When I read through my will after my diagnosis, I was pleased. What I had written before was what I still wanted.

Thinking through your possessions. Identifying those possessions that have value for us or for others may seem simple for some and challenging for others. In the retreats I lead for people facing a life-threatening situation, I often use the following exercise to help them focus on the treasured and valuable possessions they have. Try it and see if it helps you discover what items you have that you might want to leave to a specific person.

EXERCISE   Imagine that you are in your grocery store and you have just purchased your groceries. You are now headed home with your sack. When you get there, you put the items away. As you glance at the clock, you see that you miraculously have an extra forty-five minutes or so to yourself! Perhaps the kids are off doing some activity and your answering machine is on. You have the luxury of a period of solitude to do whatever you want!

You make a cup of tea and walk into the other room. The light is very beautiful and clear. As you look around, your eye begins to fall on certain things that you especially like, and you begin to go through the house room by room to savor those things you remember and love. You wander through the living room and the bedrooms. You go upstairs, and into every room.

Review your jewelry box. Look at your trophies. Open your china closet and drawers. Dare to open your basement, attic, garage . . . the places where you've stored things away forever. You feel drawn to certain things and the memories they bring.

You decide to give yourself a break and sit down. You take out a sheet of paper and write what you recall about some of your favorite things. For example, a painting purchased on a holiday with your parents, a ring inherited from your grandmother, a framed greeting card that you found inspiring, a tea set you played with as a child, a photo album, a kite your family flew at a reunion picnic. After you make your list, write beside each item the answer to this question: "Why did that item bubble up as a favorite? What is it that makes it special to me?" Be specific. For example, "So and so gave it to me," "It represents my favorite hobby," or "I remember the wonderful time when we. . . ."

Now let your mind drift lightly over all of your loved ones, and choose who you would prefer to get each item. Whose face will light up when you give this item to them? In whose home would it make you feel warm to visualize each item? Write that person's name beside the object. And then beside their name, write the reason you thought of that person to receive that gift.

Turning it into reality. After going through this exercise, you will have an appreciation of just how simple making a will can be. It can certainly be more elaborate, yet it can be as simple as this exercise. There is one caution, however. Remember that I said, "Think of a loved one"? Are there any loved ones whose names you have *not* written down beside an item? The first draft of your list will not always provide a proper match of gifts and beneficiaries. Modify this list for anyone important you may have missed the first time. Think to yourself, *What of mine would this person like to have, and why?* Do it again and again until you are satisfied that you've remembered everyone and your important things are distributed. So often I hear wives tell me they have no need for a will because their husband has one. More often than not, the items that this exercise helps to identify are not mentioned in the husband's will. If this is the case, you might consider preparing a will of your own, and designating these special items for your loved ones.

After you make your will, it is good to review it periodically. As with all legal documents, your executor and any other key people should be given a copy. Don't just put a copy in your safe deposit box, where the contents will be unavailable and unknowable, perhaps for years. Be sure that those who need to take action after you are gone have what they need in order to do it.

Three stories about wills

A long-time college friend of mine told me about her experience. Mary's mother died in a car accident while driving home late one night. Clearly it was a sudden and unexpected death. Mary comes from a small town, where her family has been in local, state, and national politics for decades. History and tradition are fundamental to her family structure. There were mementos, antiques, town property, and rural property that were part of a vast fortune befitting such a tradition. After her mother's death, Mary said that she and her two adult sisters drew lots and took turns, fairly choosing which of their mother's things each wished to claim. Yet, because the mother had not provided any specific direction for the distribution of items, none of the daughters has a specially gifted item.

A few years ago I watched a film called *The Dresser*, which had a very profound effect on me. It was about a man whose job was to dress actors in costumes for the theater before they went on to perform. He was a loyal and attentive servant and was completely devoted to one particular actor. He served the man for many years, through good and bad times. When the actor finally died, the actor had made gifts to all of his family members and other actors—but he completely ignored the man who loved him most and had been with him the longest. So often we follow the conventions of propriety: give to relatives, not friends; give to family, not charity. When you have your list of loved ones, double-check it to see that *all* the people who have meaning and significance for you are on it. Perhaps there is someone who may have cared for you for a long time but who is outside the traditional circle of recipients, someone who may be considered inconsequential. Perhaps a favorite item would have special meaning for such a person.

Another film that made a big impact on me was *An Early Frost*. A man was in the hospital, dying from AIDS. He was a man of little wealth, with little to give. Yet it was important for him, with his very few possessions, to deliver his small items ceremoniously to each person. Whether a pen, a robe, or a stage prop, he gave to each personally and deliberately. It reminded me of how we often want to do this giving when we are alive, to be able to savor that moment with the person receiving our gift of love.

And for those receiving the gifts of a friend—they must realize that refusal to accept the item when it is offered comes from a death-denying mentality. Recipients need to honor the moment and receive with grace, and without objections, when a dying person wants to give it "now." We should honor the giver in return—by giving back to the giver a verbal or nonverbal expression of gratitude.

Something often overlooked
We've discussed care and concern for our loved ones and disposition of our assets. One important area remains to be discussed, one that is commonly overlooked: our pets. Let me share with you an anecdote from my own experience, highlighting how important pets are for some of us.

I had shed very few tears regarding my diagnosis and treatments. I had a good attitude and was willing to work hard and try what was recommended. There weren't many moments of deep despair nor deep grief, but this was one. I remember having this poignant experience at home during one R & R week between treatment protocols. I was lying on my stomach in my bed with my chin cupped in my hands. I had two cats whom I loved very much. The heat in my bed came from two warm, purring bodies. Teddy was lying on the left pillow, and Flannel was on the right pillow. Our faces were within inches of each other. Suddenly I started to cry because I had handled everything about my dying so well—except for who would take care of my cats. My parents had never had cats; they were not "cat people." Nor were my friends cat people. Planning for my cats' welfare was my unfinished business.

I remember my tears and the pain in my heart as I talked to the cats out loud, asking, "Should I have you put to sleep? Should I give you to an unknown future in the shelter? Should I split you up or leave you together? What would you like me to do?" I know it sounds silly and trite, but some of you will understand. I was sincere in my dilemma.

The irony is, if they could have talked, they would have said, "Don't worry, we will die before you." Today they are both gone.

As I stated earlier, I don't have a formal estate and trust plan. Perhaps my simple approach will be helpful if you also have a small estate.

On my death, the process may be summed up as: delegate, liquidate, tithe, and distribute shares. I have directed that most of my estate will be liquidated and divided among certain parties. I have some items of sentimental value that I have exempted from the liquidation. These exempted items have been specified to be given to certain individuals. For example, there are a few items I plan to return, including a lifetime-loaned piece of artwork. There are also a few pieces of jewelry.

I have adopted the principle of tithing with my annual income, so I will continue that practice in my death. Of the amount to be distributed, I will tithe the top 10 percent to my church. Many people are considering this option today, and I encourage you to think about it. The balance will then be distributed to my designated beneficiaries.

The remaining estate will be distributed this way: I listed all of the people to whom I wanted to give something. Instead of writing an amount by each of their names, I assigned each person a number of shares. For example, some people get three shares of my estate, some two shares, and some one share, based on many variables.

Eight years have passed since the initial review of my will. As in all lives, my circumstances have changed. The share values in my estate have dropped dramatically. Yet I'm pleased that my structure is sound. It still works.

Although no people have left my life, new people have entered it. Some of the people are now rearranged in my share distribution, and although I haven't dropped any people from my list, it might be appropriate to do so in the future. I will also need to constantly check specific facts in my will; for example, is the name of my current church the name found in the will? Have I found a new charity that I didn't favor in the past?

Important Papers

When we are dying, all of us need to realize that we are not just human beings with names and a few possessions. We are also accounts, and more than accounts—PINs, codes, passwords, ID numbers, and social security numbers. To keep our affairs in order, we must be up-to-date and organized.

There are several popular organizers now; *Everything Your Heirs Need to Know,* which is an excellent book, is one. Some of the tips they provide include:

- Keep one set of papers in a fireproof box at home and readily accessible.
- Give a second set of your papers to a friend, adviser, and/or executor.

It is most important to keep the documents accessible to you and their whereabouts known to your loved ones. You might keep these in what I like to call a plan-ahead box, which I think of as a collection of my current choices and decisions. Some of the documents you might want to include in your own plan-ahead box are:

- Necessary personal data (copies of accounts for banking, credit cards, car registrations, passport, social security card)

- Legal documents (birth certificate; marriage certificate; family death certificates; military discharge papers; medical, life, house, and car insurance policies; real estate deeds; mortgage papers; the immediate past year's income taxes)
- Stocks, bonds, and securities
- Household warranties and instruction booklets
- Other important property and business papers
- Papers such as your organ donation card, a copy of the back side of your driver's license, guardianship directives, estate planning papers, will, living will, durable power of attorney for health care, and durable power of attorney for property)

It might be helpful to have a photo album containing snapshots of your most important assets, such as individual items of jewelry, electronics, or collections. Some people like to videotape their home, room by room, with close-ups of significant or favorite things. An album and video tape can also be included among your important papers. One extra bonus is that you have them available in the event of a fire or burglary to help with your insurance claims.

Deb, an associate, shared her secret, a practice from which many of us can learn. She and her husband, as an act of love for each other, review all their important documents annually on their wedding anniversary. Reviewing all their choices and decisions is a symbolic act and ritual. I recommend this.

Questions to consider

Do I want to donate organs or body parts for transplantation?

Have I signed my driver's license or organ donor card and had it witnessed?

Have I discussed my organ donation decisions with all of my loved ones?

Do I want my body used for research or experimentation?

Have all guardianship issues been resolved?
    (e.g., minors, elders, pets)

Do I want to do formal estate planning?

Would estate planning minimize taxes and maximize the inheritance for my loved ones?

Do I have a Last Will and Testament?

Is my will up-to-date?

Have I provided key individuals with a copy of my will so they will not need to access my safe deposit box to find it?

Where do I have all of my important papers?
    (e.g., Necessary personal data: medical records—living will, durable power of attorney for health care, donor card; legal papers—durable power of attorney for property; guardianship directives; insurance policies; financial records and papers,

household warranties and instructions; other important property and business papers)

Are my papers secure and in a fireproof place?

Do my loved ones know where to find my important papers without me?

6

Strains and Tensions

Thus far, we have addressed tasks that are appropriate to do without a moment's hesitation out of love and respect for our family and friends. These efforts have been appropriate for the well and the sick, for the healthy and the not so healthy. Every activity we've walked through has been preparing for "just in case."

Now we turn from the medical, ethical, legal, and financial aspects of dying, to the psychological and sociological aspects of our dying and death.

None of us can know our future. Yet we can set some expectations of what will happen. With some forethought, we will be better able to cope with what comes. By thinking ahead, we hope that we and our loved ones will be less anxious and less frustrated. Undoubtedly, many of our predictions will not occur, and many surprises will come. But after this time of speculating, we will better deal with the inevitable strains and tensions of a lingering death.

What will our feelings, thoughts, and behaviors be on this trip of trips?

Here are three stressful areas from a dying person's point of view. They include general fears, unfinished business, and quitter's guilt. Following these, you'll find tensions from the loved ones' point of view, which include acceptance of our dying, the subject of food, and not knowing when the patient will die.

Fears   Most people fear dying more than death itself. Specific fears include:

- Pain—increasing, intolerable pain
- Awareness of our deterioration and the humiliation of decline
- Sense of loss of what we were before
- Loss of control and inability to take care of ourselves
- Dependency on others for our physical needs
- Dying, the moment of transition itself: Is it an ending or a beginning?

Earlier, I mentioned that for a difficult journey I pack a care package. In my care package I include Scripture, song, and symbols.

I have discovered a wonderful place in the book of Luke, chapter 20, verses 27-38, where Jesus declared that God is "not the God of the dead, but of the living." The point he was making was that, since God is called "God of Abraham, Isaac" and so forth, these ancestors, dead centuries ago, are not dead, but living. Jesus was arguing his case for resurrection. And I, too, believe that God cares not only for our seventy-plus years on Earth, but through eternity.

Finally, regarding fear, I am indebted to Dan Lupton, an executive with the Chapel of the Air Ministries. He has taught me that God says "Fear not" more times than anything else in the Bible. From Genesis through Revelation we can hear that command, appeal, and encouragement.

Unfinished Business

A person with a life-threatening illness generally realizes that he or she is going to die soon. But death may not be imminent. Many people find that they are waiting for an important event to happen before they die.

Perhaps you have known patients who have had strong impulses to maintain their abilities as long as possible. They might say, "I can't go on that medication until . . ." or "I can't take that treatment because. . . ." We have all heard stories of people who said, "I know that I am sick, but I can't/won't die until. . . ." The "because" and "until" are important to the patient. Sometimes caregivers get upset with this language and behavior.

But the patient knows what is important for him or her: to see a child graduate, to celebrate a parent's eightieth birthday, to attend a retirement party, or to witness the birth of a grandchild. Very often, once the event or milestone passes, the patient dies.

Bill was a great example of this determination.

Bill refused to die until his and his wife's dream house was built. They had planned it as their retirement home. They had decided to stay in the community where they had worked and where their families lived—not to move to a warmer climate as many retirees do. However, Bill was diagnosed with primary liver cancer during the construction of their dream house.

They had the creativity and the means to design the dream house to fit them comfortably for the rest of their lives. It was well thought out, including wheelchair accessibility and living quarters for a resident caregiver. But mostly, the house was designed to accommodate their loving relationship and their gracious hospitality for family and friends. The home was nestled in a woods and prairie setting, with cathedral ceilings, skylights for observing the stars and moon, and lots of windows for bird watching.

When Bill was diagnosed, his disease was far along. He asked the architect how long it would take to get the walls up and the roof on. He then vowed that he would not die until he and his wife moved in.

I remember a difficult but poignant moment. He participated fully in the construction of the house, but he refused to pick the wallpaper for the bedroom and dressing area. He insisted that his wife pick it. He knew that he would never live there and that it had to suit her.

Bill actually did live long enough to move in. He died in their new home.

Evon is another example of someone surviving to fulfill a goal. She was diagnosed with primary lung cancer. Evon ran a family business and, in her later days, worked from her home on oxygen, pulling the tank from room to room.

As Evon's health deteriorated, she went back to the hospital. I drove to see her on an Easter Sunday after church. I wanted to bring her Easter flowers and, in my own quiet way, the message of Easter.

That afternoon, Evon recalled that she wasn't sure whether she had been baptized as a child. As we talked, it became clear that it was terribly important for her to be baptized. The hospital chaplain baptized her that Easter Sunday night. She died the next morning.

People tease me that my own unfinished business is this book. But I don't believe that. Consequently, I have learned that we can't speculate on another's unfinished business! But it is important to inquire of a dying patient if there is any unfinished business and to help him or her complete it.

One of the most difficult areas of stress revolves around the patient's sense of guilt. When the patient is struggling with the acceptance of his decline, self-blame can occur: *I didn't exercise enough, or the chemo would have taken better; I didn't do enough creative visualizations; I should have eaten better; I should have prayed harder; I shouldn't give up.* **Quitter's Guilt**

More than likely, the loved ones are not blaming. But they are grieving. Sometimes the inner dialogue continues: *If I don't continue with treatment, I will disappoint them. They will think I'm a quitter. And if I disappoint them, they will withdraw their love.*

Sometimes the inner dialogue becomes a literal dialogue. Tensions escalate, and loved ones exclaim, "Try harder!" And patients yell, "Don't leave me all alone!"

Marilou, my friend and bookseller, introduced me to the work of May Sarton. Well known for her poetry and fiction, Sarton is perhaps best known for her published letters and journals. Writing about her mother's illness and death, she reflected: **Acceptance of Our Dying**

> *All I wish is to sit for a long time silent and alone and just be still and try to be reborn again, for I have been dying with mother for so long.*

With my own illness, there have been several big scares that have allowed my loved ones to do most of their anticipatory grieving. We've been through all of the classic phases described by Elizabeth Kubler-Ross: denial, anger, bargaining, depression, and acceptance. Since she first offered her model over twenty years ago, others have added layers of sophistication. Yet no one has substantially changed her concept.

I have gone through the volatile passages and so have my family and close friends. I can tell you first-hand it is incredibly painful to watch others respond to our illness. Fortunately, I don't think my family will have to go through those phases again.

Food

When a person is dying, caregivers and loved ones want the patient to eat. Eat, eat, eat. Breakfast, lunch and dinner. "Eat your meat. Eat your vegetables. You must eat; you must have your energy."

However, a dying person often loses appetite. As a result, caregivers instinctively insist on feeding the patient. Feeding is an expression of love. However, when the patient rejects the food, the caregiver often feels personally rejected. Badgering questions ensue: "Didn't I do it right?" "Are the pieces too big? too small?" The caregiver's motto, "You Must Eat to Live," is no longer shared by the patient.

On this most private journey, the patient is no longer experiencing living but is instead experiencing dying.

When the Patient Will Die

God doesn't tell you when you are going to die, because he wants it to be a big surprise.—Alan, age 7

Not knowing the time of our death causes heightened tension everywhere. Relatives come from far away to "wait it out." There's often an incredible frustration in our loved ones' eyes. Their lives cannot remain on hold. Spouses have to work; there are important meetings to attend; a child's birthday party needs to be planned; people are anxious to get on with their lives.

Expect strains and tensions. They can't be ignored. But they can be dealt with. In retrospect they will appear less overwhelming than at the beginning. Everyone involved will be grateful that you faced these difficult issues.

Questions to consider

What strains and tensions do I expect to surface in my dying process?

    (e.g., fears, regrets, frustrations)

What "unfinished business" do I want to finish before I die?

    (e.g., complete a project, witness a family milestone)

7

Good-byes, Forgiveness, and Blessings

Unfortunately, many times saying good-bye happens too late—it happens at a wake when your loved ones are filing by your body, perhaps bending to kiss your forehead.

The phrase "letting go" is often used in our decline and death. I'm told that I can expect that I won't need much coaching to let go, that for most of us, we let go intuitively—that during this process we are almost on automatic pilot.

Letting Go and Saying Good-bye

I learned the phrase "saying good-bye" from Judy Tatelbaum, author and counselor, when she led a workshop at a National Hospice Organization's annual meeting. She shared a point of view that was new to me, one I now appreciate. I now know that it is up to the dying one to initiate saying good-bye.

More often than not, the patient accepts her death sooner than her loved ones do. Death itself doesn't frighten me. My beliefs help me feel like I'm being offered a "cut in line" at the theater by the usher, that I'm being led into the preferred seating section. If this is a common thought, then we patients can afford to be generous. We can give our loved ones a gift, a caring act that may be labeled "letting go and saying good-bye."

I know I will be letting go and saying good-bye to feelings and holidays, places, things, circles of friends, and intimates. First to go will be **feelings and holidays.** I remember saying to myself, *This is my last Christmas,* with some sadness and sorrow. Palm Sunday has been my favorite Sunday. Palm Sunday tells the story of Jesus facing his death. He was prepared.

On the Palm Sunday before I thought I would die, I experienced a wonderful service on two levels. On one level, I was in the balcony of a large Gothic church and looking down on the upturned faces of delighted children processing down the center aisle with their huge palm fronds. There was exuberance, energy, and pomp. I was sad, thinking that I would never see that pageant again. Yet on the other level I was excited, because maybe there's even more pomp and pageantry with angels soon to come!

There may be good-byes to **places.** Some people will miss a second home. For many people it will be a favorite golf course or a spot where they sat to watch the sunset. I loved the movie *The Trip to Bountiful,* where the live-in mother-in-law suddenly disappears and makes a trip to her childhood home to say good-bye.

We will say good-bye to **things.** Sometimes saying good-bye to things means handing them over to a loved one for their continued use or care. Remember wandering through our home with a cup of tea when we recorded our things for our loved ones? There's a great final scene in the movie *Citizen Kane*. Do you remember hearing "Rosebud"? Rosebud was the name of the young lad's most prized possession.

Saying good-bye to **friendships** and circles of friends takes time. We begin to let go of our least important friends first—people we know from work or through our hobbies and avocations, recreation groups, church groups. We gradually decrease those we interact with as we focus more and more inward. Eventually we are surrounded only by our **intimates**—our closest family members, friends, and pets.

Saying good-bye to intimates can be the most difficult, because we experience so keenly their anticipatory grief in addition to what we are experiencing ourselves.

One way to say good-bye is to do what Bob Greene, the nationally syndicated columnist, suggests. With his sister, he wrote the book *To Our Children's Children*. With guided questions, they prompt our memory and encourage us to record the history of our life so our loved ones can better remember where we came from, what we did, and who we are.

There are other gestures we can undertake to temper this grief also. We can leave behind some loving mementos for our intimates. Consider writing a letter, keeping a journal, making a videotape, assembling a scrapbook, or completing a photo album.

Forgiveness

In saying good-bye, it is appropriate and provides better closure to seek and give forgiveness.

Saying good-bye is a time for careful and sometimes painful self-examination. As you recall people you've known, names of some that you would want to forgive appear from your past. We can take action to contact those people and to set the situation straight. Similarly, we have the opportunity to seek forgiveness. The time of our dying is also a time when others seek to "clean the slate" with us as well. Saying good-bye is a powerful opportunity to grant forgiveness for old injuries.

I encountered the theme of forgiveness late in life. The reason was a broken heart. Most teens have a round or two of broken hearts during their high school years. But I had a delay in this area of personal growth. Lewis Smedes, in *Forgive and Forget: Healing the Hurts We Don't Deserve,* offers insight that helped me during the past and that I'm sure will help me again in the future. Responding to how people forgive, he offers, "slowly . . . with a little understanding . . . in confusion . . . with anger left over . . . a little at a time . . . freely, or not at all."

One word of caution. It is very important that your family realize just how critical this exchange of forgiveness and good-byes is. Some families have a protector at the door whose job is to keep out "trouble," thinking it will disturb the dying person unnecessarily to face old hostilities or grievances. That person may sometimes be heard to say, "Just who do you think you are, coming here like this!" or "Where do you get the gall . . . ?" What I have learned, and what I encourage you to express to others, is that these types of encounters, between people who have been at odds over the years, have the potential to be some of the most beautiful moments in their lives. Note that I said "have the potential." Unfortunately it doesn't always work that way.

Do you know a story of a long hostility that was mended on a deathbed? Let me share two stories I know. One was between a daughter and a mother. The daughter needed to tell her mother before her mother's death, "Mother, you know I had an abortion, and I know you know I had one. I gave up a baby and you never had a grandchild. Can you forgive me?" In fact, the mother already had. However, the dialogue brought a healing closure to the relationship.

In another story, a son came back home to his father, who was dying, and said, "I know you've always been ashamed that I dropped out of college, that I have not been a professional like you, that I didn't continue the family name with prestige and power." The father said, "That time is long over. You've given me pride because your hands have created works of beauty. It took me decades to appreciate your vocation." The healing in this relationship was also a thing of beauty. It is precisely for these reasons that *we must let the patient—not the spouse, the parent, the well-intentioned friend, nor the child—decide who can come in or who must stay out.* Only the patient should control who is allowed to enter the room and who is turned away. The patient is the only person who can grant, or receive, forgiveness. You, as a patient, might be able to identify someone in your inner circle who can help this happen for you.

Blessings

One ritual that has helped me with these painful moments of saying good-bye is a process that many Jews and Christians adopt. It is giving a blessing to those we love.

In their book *The Blessing,* Gary Smalley and John Trent tell of the way that Isaac blessed Jacob and Esau from his deathbed.

Giving blessings is a way to make an imprint on our loved ones' lives. To bless a person is simply to call him or her by name and affirm, acknowledge, and encourage that loved one, bringing out what is good and valuable within them. Most of us will have the opportunity and privilege to grant blessings to those we love. The question is, will we?

Here's my story of saying good-bye, seeking forgiveness, and giving blessings. I had a small camel-colored leather address book that I loved very much. The cover was warm and worn in the way that fine glove leather gets over time, and I loved to slide my fingertips over it, both for the feel of it and for the knowledge that within it were the names of so many beautiful and treasured friends. The pages were of a very fine pale blue linen, smooth and sheer and embossed with die-cut letters. As I thumbed through the pages they crinkled slightly. I can hear that sound even now. One day I was at home in bed. It was during one of my R & Rs from the hospital, and I was getting weaker and sicker. I remember turning each page and sliding my finger down to each name and pausing as I thought of each one. I wondered, *When I die, will I regret not having repaired some aspect of our relationship?* I was searching my heart to see if I was in good standing with each. I needed to see if I was out of sorts with anyone. This was not a superficial "I want to clean up my act." I genuinely did not want to die without trying to repair anything still unresolved. No book told me to do it. It simply became a gut-wrenching imperative because I was convinced that I would die soon.

There were over one hundred names in that address book—associates, college friends, a few people I was dating or had dated. And as I slid my finger carefully down each page, there were only two names where I stopped. Only two, where I knew in my heart, I had something to do.

That night, with very shaky hands and voice, I dialed those two phone numbers. For each one the message was the same. And I had to get it out hurriedly—I didn't want a dialogue! I was crying inside. Yet I forced myself to tell each, "It's very important for me to tell you I love you. Please listen; please hear me. I have loved you; I will always love you." Although the message for each was similar, the reason for each call was different. In one I was seeking forgiveness, and in the other I was offering forgiveness. I know that I slept better that night, having tackled that difficult deed.

The following week I was back in the hospital, and my parents came to visit. I had been crying. They inquired why, then asked who I had talked to. When they found out, they directed the hospital to prohibit the caller from calling back.

What my dear parents didn't realize, in their wish to protect me, was that my tears were an incredible outpouring of relief, for the caller had called to seek forgiveness, and I had the opportunity to give a blessing.

It is so very important to seek and give forgiveness. These actions won't make things right. They won't make everything "nice" or "happy." They are simply acts of care and compassion, as painful as they may be.

Questions to consider

To whom do I want to say good-bye?

How do I want to say good-bye?

What am I doing to prepare my loved ones for their grieving when I am gone?
   (e.g., tailor-made "gifts of love," personal letters, journals, photo albums, scrapbooks, videotapes)

What forgiveness do I want to give?

What forgiveness do I want to receive?

What blessings do I want to give?

What blessings do I want to receive?

8

Final
Moments

This "trip of trips" will have a departure date and gate. Not knowing, literally, what it will be like, I hope it will be calm. In my own travels, I've had various experiences before departure. For example, I've seen the boarding light flashing and have waited a long time to get on the plane, becoming impatient, bored, and frustrated for many minutes. Other times I've been out of breath from hurrying down the terminal corridors trying to catch a flight, when I was worried that I wouldn't make it. And many times I have realized that I was overburdened with too much luggage to get on board easily. And once I had a serious fright, wondering if I had forgotten my passport.

What Will Happen?

Like many people, I have always wanted to know what it will feel like to die. How does the nervous system work at the moment of death? What happens in the brain at the moment of death? How do muscles work at that moment? I deliberately looked for an answer. And no one would give me a straight answer. Some people said cavalierly, "Oh, no one knows." Others said with a smirk, "No one's come back to tell us."

I asked one doctor, who told me to ask another doctor, who said to ask the academics and researchers. I was pushed further and further from the medical caregivers, toward the more remote and dispassionate scientists. I felt chastised for asking such a question. But I still wanted to know! During this time I was working for a friend and client in Montreal. His company had made reservations for me at the Ritz Hotel on Sherbrooke—a very classy place. After a dinner with him, I decided to take a stroll through the neighborhood galleries and boutiques. It was a beautiful summer evening. Many people from the city come there to browse. I found a French and English bookstore and went in to see what was on its shelves. I looked through the health books in the English section and purchased *The Way We Die*, written by two Canadian physicians.

I went back to the hotel. When I arrived, my bed had been turned down and there were Godiva chocolates on the pillow. So I climbed into bed and curled up to read. The answers were there. I took great comfort from reading that book.

From hospice training, I know that there are symptoms of imminent death caregivers can spot: cold feet, a rattle in the respiratory tract. But I wasn't interested in the symptoms perceived by those on the outside looking in; I wanted to know what I would experience from the inside, looking out.

What I gathered from the book was that our system closes down at the end, in a pattern, almost like sea waves breaking. As our system begins to close down, the waves roll in, one on top of the next, building toward "the big wave." Sets of smaller waves are followed by a much bigger one. Surfers and seamen know this sequence.

This gave me the imagery to visualize the moment of my death. I envision my system as having a very protective first rolling wave where the nerve endings will close down. My consciousness will become more and more inward. The tidal rhythm will remove sensations before the "big wave" comes in. I will have a self-protective device in my body.

As a management consultant, I've coached managers and executives on their oral presentations. As a speaker myself, I know that being nervous is normal as we approach an engagement. I'm not ashamed to be nervous or scared before a major event. I think there's a parallel to dying. We can use the tricks of the speaking trade to deal with the fear of dying. Here are two favorites that I find helpful. **Fearful of Dying?**

> *One.* Visualize success. Visualize what happens *after* you are done. If we anticipate the applause/reward/affirmation that will be on the other side of the event, we can usually get over the hurdle.

> *Two.* Grow quiet. Get centered and focused. Just visualize something very calming. We might remember a beautiful sonata or concerto or an image of a landscape. For me it's always water. I imagine driving up a winding drive, heading north along the northern California and Oregon coast. I never know what's around each bend, but I'm always trusting that I'll round it safely. As I move along, my eye catches the incredible vast beauty of the ocean, and I gasp with awe.

We have a wonderful variety of literature, art, and music that can help us prepare also—through calming us, giving us encouraging images on which to dwell.

Psalm 121 is the first place I go for comfort. When I go here I have no need to go further:

> *I lift up my eyes to the hills—*
> *where does my help come from?*
> *My help comes from the LORD,*
> *the Maker of heaven and earth.*
> *He will not let your foot slip—*
> *he who watches over you will not slumber;*
> *indeed, he who watches over Israel*
> *will neither slumber nor sleep.*
> *The LORD watches over you—*
> *the LORD is [beside you];*
> *the sun will not harm you by day,*
> *nor the moon by night.*
> *The LORD will keep you from all harm—*
> *he will watch over your life;*
> *the LORD will watch over your coming*
> *and going*
> *both now and forevermore.*

Whom Do You Want with You? Many people like to think about the moment of their passing as a time when they will be surrounded by those they love. I certainly hope that will be true, although it's not something we can take for granted.

Some people find it easy to identify the loved ones they would want with them. Others might say only who they *don't* want. In dying, as in life, there are people who are troublesome, who don't contribute to a peaceful or positive atmosphere. Perhaps anyone's presence at the time of death should be by invitation only. I mentioned earlier the value of forgiving and giving blessings. During these final moments, however, the person who is dying should be respected, a "Do Not Enter" sign placed on the door if he or she wishes, and only select people invited to the bedside.

It's helpful to visualize who you might want with you. I was once led on a directed visualization where the facilitator asked us this question: "What is the ideal for you?"

Visualize the Moment

I have friends and loved ones in many places and from different periods of my life. My visualization included many of these friends who would give me comfort if they were with me at that moment. But realistically, it would not be reasonable to expect many of these people to be in the same room at the same time!

I'm glad I have the dramatist's license to choreograph a show that will never be produced! My visualization comforted and reassured me. With it, I knew that there were people who would come to wish me well if they could.

If you have strong feelings about those who should or should not be present, circulate those desires through your grapevine. You'll increase the chances that your wishes will be honored.

I have been fascinated to learn, in my readings and travels, of the many cultural and tribal customs and traditions surrounding the moment of death. Customs include making a circle and chanting, burning incense, and pulsating drumming. Most customs center around one principle: Those gathered are sending messages of "bon voyage" and "fare thee well" to the person dying.

The Sacred Art of Dying

As a child, I remember taking a Caribbean cruise with my parents, in 1960. As we cruised south out of New York City, it was a true Noel Coward/Cole Porter experience. The band played; confetti was thrown; families waved as the ship pulled out of the dock.

Although death is not honored with such zeal and noise in our culture, various religious groups have their own prayers and rites of transition. Some rites are not formal, yet seem appropriate for the moment. Many people have said to a loved one just before their death, "It's okay. Let go. Go on." It's as if the loved one needed just that little permission to be set free. Many have died immediately after such encouragement. My friend Terry told me of her experience in holding her dear friend Dempsey's feet, as he was dying, and spontaneously singing to him the song "Going Home." These are moments of great personal intimacy.

Experts have told us that hearing is one of the last senses to fail. When you gather around a dying loved one, make sounds, even if you have nothing to say. Let your loved one hear your tone and rhythm. I like to think that at the moment of my passing, the heartfelt song of a loved one will carry me on.

I was surprised to hear of studies made, by hospice professionals, on when people actually die. Some people die when loved ones are in the room; others wait until their loved ones are absent. Many caregivers who have been in close attendance risk their own health to guarantee that they will be there with their loved one at the moment of death. They don't sleep; they don't eat; they risk permanent bladder damage; they just won't leave the bedside. Then after a long period of this behavior, when they simply must leave and they do, the loved one dies. The caregivers become upset and won't forgive themselves for taking that necessary personal time.

But many professionals maintain that the timing of death is actually the choice of the individual. And the individual may choose the moment with thoughtfulness for the people who are present. Some may wish to spare loved ones the actual moment. Will I want to be in the company of others or alone? I don't know. I trust the people close to me will accept whatever happens. Since I've preferred my own company for some major trips in my life, I wouldn't be surprised if my death turns out to be a solo affair.

We reach a time in our dying process when we consider where we would like to be when we die.

Where Do You Want to Be?

In our dying, each of us wants a place of comfort. Yet we must resist projecting our own values on the one who is dying and defer to him or her. Patients have little control over any aspect of their lives. They need to feel control whenever they can, and especially over this question. They should be allowed to choose the location that is comfortable for them.

Home. Many people are strong proponents for dying at home, assuming that it is a place of comfort, and cozy, when in reality it might not be. There are many legitimate reasons a person would not want to die at home.

I know of one man who didn't want to die in his marital bed. He didn't want his corpse in that bed to be the last memory of his soon-to-be widow. Another example is a widow who didn't want to die at home because there was no one there anymore. In both situations, their caregivers assumed that home was the best place, yet it wasn't.

However, being at home *is* a comfortable choice for many. They are in the midst of favorite things, memories, and loved ones—connected to as much normalcy as possible.

Nursing Homes. Another site is the nursing home. Nursing homes frequently have a path of progression to different places in the facility, depending on the patient's condition.

Hospitals. For some, the hospital is the preferred place. There are usually specific rooms for terminal patients, where comfort and care, not heroic efforts, are the norm. These rooms are decorated warmly and have a bedroom or sitting-room look. Often a comfortable recliner chair, pullout sofa, or studio bed is there for overnight companions.

Hospice Care. Hospice isn't always a place—it's a concept. Hospice is a caring community of professionals and volunteers who support the dying person. Hospice workers are committed to caring for us and our loved ones by helping us remain in control, whether we are in our homes, nursing homes, or hospitals. Hospice care also offers an additional benefit. Bereavement counseling, should your loved ones wish it, is available for a year after your death.

I was privileged to go to the original hospice, St. Christopher's Hospice, near London, founded by Cecily Saunders. It's a two-story building set in a tree-lined neighborhood with a patio garden surrounding it. The building has extra-large windows and even has a preschool on the first floor, full of young children. All generations are there. It is a place full of laughter and smiles, and there is a true community feeling.

I'm concerned that hospice might lose its "caring community" aspect and become more of a health care economic reform movement. Yet one positive change I have seen since my own diagnosis is a far greater leniency to accept single patients who do not have a parent or other relative caregiver nearby. Several years ago, I was saddened that I didn't qualify for hospice care because my parents lived in another state and I had no immediate family. Today, a loving friend qualifies as a hospice caregiver. I'm immensely grateful for that change.

When you consider where to spend your last days (presuming you will have a choice), it is very important to express your thoughts, wishes, and values to your loved ones. What are your objectives? What are your concerns? Let your family, social workers, and health care professionals help you find the solution that will accommodate your particular circumstances. I absolutely want hospice care. It is the solution for me.

I remember going on a trip with my parents to Great Britain. It was a holiday in the countryside. We were driving in the southwest of England, through a lovely narrow-laned district. We stopped for a stretch and went to walk in an old church cemetery nearby.

My mother and I share this interest in browsing old church cemeteries. We were walking through, reading the markers, reading aloud the limericks, looking at the family names, always half-hoping that we would find the unusual name of my mother's family, which is Foy.

My father is not fond of this pastime, so he walked around and found the belfry. He quickly came to fetch us to see a group of people who were going to pull the bells. When we asked why they were ringing the bells, they said there was to be a wedding very soon. It was a very rural place. People began coming down the dirt paths—ladies with hats, little boys with vests, one boy riding a tricycle. We didn't want to go in the church, but we did want to see the bride and groom.

I remember standing and looking at the gathered faces from the side door. It was an unusual view of the crowd. I noticed especially how everyone stood. Waves of men and women in each pew turned to watch the bride process down the aisle. A full congregation of men and women rose and witnessed the bride walking down the aisle to join her groom.

It was a perfect metaphor for my vision of hospice care. I value the men and women of hospice as people who want to witness my journey to join God. Hospice families and communities do not turn their heads nor shy away from the dying, nor from death. They will rise and bless me onward, as the congregation did with the bride. I really want people like that with me.

I don't know *where* yet. It may be home, a hospital, nursing home, or a hospice center. But for now, I like my own bedroom.

Famous Last Words

It is written that Beethoven, on his way to death, said, "I shall hear in Heaven." In *They Went That-A-Way*, Malcolm Forbes describes the last words of Babe Ruth:

> That evening, at 6:45, he suddenly got up out of bed and started to walk across the room. The doctor led him back to bed and asked, "Where are you going, Babe?" Ruth replied, "I'm going over the valley." At 7:30 P.M., he fell into a coma, and a half hour later, he died.

Our last words are not necessarily famous, but they are often remembered by our loved ones and might specially reflect our life or character. But I don't have a clue as to what will come from my lips. My hope is to live in such a way that these words, written by Dagens Nyheter, could be said of me:

> The day you were born, everybody was happy—you cried alone. Make your life such, that in your last hour, all others are weeping, and you are the only one without a tear to shed! Then you shall calmly face death, whenever it comes.

Rites of Transition

Not having been raised in the Roman Catholic tradition, I remember my initial response to hearing of people having Last Rites. From movies, I had a cynical view of robed priests, commissioned to give Last Rites to the dying. It was as if the priest were the person empowered to say, "Go."

Now I know better; it is often the wish of a dying person to receive a blessing. And we wish to receive that blessing with a familiar custom. Our loved ones also want to help us on our journey to heaven. Some call a priest to provide that blessing.

Today I am a member of an Episcopal church community. We have *The Book of Common Prayer* that I hold in my hands every Sunday. When I was very sick, I turned to the Last Rites section and became enamored with the beauty of the poetry on those pages.

I want those words said for me.

Questions to Consider

What do I expect to happen to me—physically, emotionally, and spiritually—during my final moments?

Whom do I want with me when I die?

Whom don't I want with me when I die?

Where do I want to be—home, hospital, nursing home, hospice?

What "rites of transition" do I want as I am dying? (e.g., prayers, songs, religious rituals)

9

Funerals

What would you think if you were handed an envelope that said, "Open when appropriate; here are my plans for my funeral"?

Some advantages of written instructions are:

- In a time of sadness and stress, it is easier to follow an action plan.
- Your loved ones won't be wondering if they honored your wishes.

Potential disadvantages of written instructions are:

- In the middle of the crisis and commotion, your loved ones might be angry and feel trapped in honoring your wishes.
- The loved ones receiving the instructions may not be financially, emotionally, or physically capable of implementing the plan.

With reference to heroic efforts and organ donation, we think primarily of the patient's needs. Now
we ask ourselves, *For whom is the funeral or memorial
service?* When I ask this question I usually hear, "That's
a silly question—it's for those left behind." But, from
a spiritual point of view, the funeral details can also be
important for the deceased.

Practically speaking, there's a blending of objectives. Funerals are important because they honor the
deceased *and* comfort those who are left behind.

Planning ahead and communicating your thoughts
will provide support for your loved ones at a difficult
time. You will also be providing yourself with a formal
activity to acknowledge and deal with your own grief.
Funeral planning, when shared by you and your loved
ones, can be one of the most powerful communication
events. Everyone has an opportunity to become closer
and accept the fact that you will, indeed, die.

Many loved ones feel better when they have a part
in shaping your funeral plans, also. They may want to
add elements for their own benefit.

**Communi-
cating Your
Wishes**

If I were to be given such an envelope, I would pray
for the courage to say to the person, "Thank you for
writing it. I want to read it now. I want to understand
it, and I want to discuss whether I can carry out your
wishes."

I'd like to share my own plans with you, my wishes
as of today. Why would I want to share something so
personal? To prove that this difficult thinking and
decision making and documenting *can* be done. I continue to learn and grow and to change my mind. The
best we can do is to update our wishes regularly so
that they reflect our current thinking when our time
comes.

There are two important aspects of planning our
funerals that happen after we have identified our preferences. The first is communication of our wishes to

those who need to know. The second is verification that our plans *can* be carried out—that our loved ones are up to it emotionally and that our plans are consistent with our church's policies and practices.

I learned the hard way how important this is.

Review your plans with your family. Although I had written my ideal plan, I had not shared it with my parents. I realized it was my responsibility, and I was aware of the benefits, yet I lacked the courage to share my plans with them.

Because I was in the middle of my illness, sharing my wishes could have had an emotional double whammy. If I presented my wishes to my parents, they might perceive that I was giving up, and, with my discussions of death, I might add to my parents' sorrow. I didn't want to burden them with what they might see as bad news.

I took comfort that I had my plans and that some friends who were more emotionally distant had my plans, just in case. But I held my sealed envelope in my fireproof box.

Not only did I have my plans but I was using them as a handout at various seminars and speaking engagements—still without my parents ever having seen them. Well, one day I got embarrassed—very embarrassed.

I was invited to do an all-day workshop for a statewide conference for the hospices of South Carolina. My parents lived a short distance away in North Carolina and had offered to pick me up and take me to their home to spend the evening. I had invited them to the seminar, to come any time they wished.

I had gone through several of the seminar's modules and was discussing the importance of communication in funeral planning, when the side door near the front of the large hall opened to my left, and I saw the conference hostess ushering my parents into the room.

It would have been bad manners not to acknowledge any new people, so I interrupted myself and proudly announced, "Please welcome my parents, Jayne and Jess—my future designated hospice caregivers." But, oh, the timing! They were ushered into the first row of seats. Just as they sat down, they were handed the then-current set of handouts, the title of which was, "Funeral Wishes of Amy Harwell." I don't remember how many shades of scarlet I turned. I don't remember giving or sustaining any eye contact with them either, nor any significant discussion of my wishes in the car afterward. I was so embarrassed that I would dare share my funeral plans with the world before I told them. I am a prime example of how we just don't talk about these things with our loved ones.

Since then, my parents and my friends have all had the opportunity to review and comment on my plans—which I have modified and adapted based on those discussions.

Review your plans with your clergy. I highly recommend that you share your plans and wishes with your clergy to see if what you want may be done. I remember leading a weekend workshop on living and dying for members of my church group. My friend and minister, Rick, called when he heard that we were going to include a discussion of spiritual matters. He asked if he could attend that portion. I responded warmly, saying that we would also be discussing funeral plans, and I asked him to do a live commentary on mine.

I distributed my plan and gave everyone some quiet time to read it. Then I asked Rick what he thought of it. I remember his response: first a smile, then a turn of his head, followed by an awkward chuckle, and the reply, "It's nice, but. . . . "

When I asked him to elaborate, he said that much of what I wanted was, by policy, unacceptable in our

Episcopal tradition. I remember his telling us that two of my wishes could not be carried out. I wanted certain songs to be sung, and I wanted an abundance of flowers to be displayed.

Episcopal tradition seeks to de-emphasize wealth and poverty in its services. Since the wealthy can afford great floral displays and the poor cannot, flowers are prohibited from the sanctuary in which services are held. After some brainstorming and discussion with Rick, we agreed that whatever flowers I wanted, I could have them in the narthex, but not in the sanctuary.

As to the music, the minister's objection to my songs was an honorable one. My choices were not in our hymnal, and he didn't want to violate the copyright laws by photocopying handouts from other books. So I did an "end run" that has benefited everyone in our church; every year I donate to my church a Christian copyright license that permits us to legally sing and make copies of my favorite songs. Not only my favorite songs, but also 90 percent of all the Christian music that is available. It is an insurance policy for my funeral service that I renew annually!

There have been some joyful by-products of this insurance policy. To the delight of all, during our well-known and well-revered custom of singing while parishioners go to the communion rail, our selections for beautiful and moving music are now vastly increased. I have had another private joy also. Recently, I attended the memorial service for twin infants. The parents had picked their favorite hymns, all of which were used, and not one of them was in our hymnal.

The following questions reflect the experience of friends, and they also result from my attending many meetings and seminars on funeral planning. Each question is also included in the workbook section in the back, with room for you to record your own thoughts and ideas.

Funeral Planning Checklist

I recognize that there are numerous traditions and customs in religions around the world and within Christian denominations. The following sequence represents my best attempt to consolidate the many elements and possibilities.

Let me encourage you to jot down any thoughts that come your way. They might be helpful for putting your wishes into that envelope and eventually sharing the envelope with your trusted loved ones.

Whom do I want to be notified of my death? Have I prepared a list so my survivors can do this easily? Depending on what type of service(s) you expect to have, you may want to make a list for each one or create a system of notification right in your address book. You may remember that I talked about my small address book with over a hundred names in it. I took some time and went through it, person by person, and indicated, by a combination of circles, stars, and asterisks, those who should be invited to my funeral and those who should simply be notified after my death.

Why would we want people to know that we have died? Probably because their love and support have been helpful on our journey. There's a tradeoff, however. As with a wedding invitation, people may feel they are obligated to attend our service or make a donation.

I was struck by the value of preparing such a list when I received an unexpected notice from Europe. A close friend of a man who had been in one of my business seminars sent me a note to tell me of John's passing. He had died of AIDS. The note had quite an impact. First, I felt guilty because I had not known John was ill, although he had clearly made a choice not to include me among his supporters. But then, because I had received the note, I was empowered to honor John by praying for him and his loved ones.

I need to resume the habit of updating my list. Last year I updated my Christmas card list. My next step is to redo my notification codes on the list. Then I will make copies of the list and give them to my loved ones. From now on, every Christmas when I go through my card list, I will be reminded to update my funeral notice list as well. I'll also put a copy of this list into my fireproof box.

What type of announcement or notification would I like to have sent to people? Have I discussed this with my loved ones? The note announcing John's death was a very simply stated, hand-written note prepared by John's friend. Far more elaborate are the funeral cards, used in some Christian denominations, that are distributed at wakes and services. The design of formal cards often includes a verse of Scripture, a line of poetry, or a personal statement. The stationery varies greatly as well. One card I recently saw had on it a line etching of Jenny, the young woman who had died.

I've made the list, but not the note. Because the note comes from the surviving loved ones, I believe it should be designed to represent their purposes and personalities.

Is there a special outfit I want to be buried in? For people who wish to have an open casket, the clothes they are buried in become important. It can be a tremendous healing experience when family and friends discuss the choice of outfit. I love the scene in the film *Long Time Companion* where the friends pick the casket costume. They remember shared laughter, pains, and aggravations and finally settle on an outfit that best symbolizes their friend. Selecting what to wear can be healing for those who choose a closed casket as well. I don't have a preferred outfit, but I look good in peaches and purples!

What do I want to have with me in my casket, if I have one? Because I hadn't attended many funerals, and knowing that I was very seriously ill, I went to my small town's funeral parlor and asked the director, Wally, for an education. He gave me a tour of his facilities.

Wally told me that family members bring a variety of things to be buried with the deceased. I had flashes of King Tut and grave robbers. People put a variety of items in caskets, including golf balls, a personal Bible, or five dollars for the horse races. Some people include a rosary, a locket, or a picture of a loved one; or for a child, a baby rattle or favorite blanket.

Wally kindly told me the story of his own high-school-age son, who had died that year in a tragic swimming accident. His family took things from the boy's bedroom, including a favorite flannel shirt and a stuffed animal, and placed them in his casket.

In the Jewish tradition, the deceased is buried covered by his tallis or prayer shawl.

I have no special requests for my casket.

Are the details necessary for my obituary readily available? Death and dying seminars often include an exercise on writing our obituary. What we write in such an exercise reflects our life values. It can become a path that guides our life. It's a technique similar to one included in many life and career path seminars.

One of the first things your survivors are asked to do, following your death, is to provide your local newspaper with information for your obituary. It's very helpful for you to put together, in one place, all the documents that would make it easy. You might include such things as your birth certificate, names and addresses of family members, important biographical facts, or your military record. If you write your obituary yourself, you have the opportunity to include the things you prefer to mention or be remembered for.

An obituary is actually just a personal biography, like a resume. Some people may think it is morbid, morose, or above the call of duty to write their obituaries. However, if you think about it, you can see that it's about details you know better than anyone else.

Much of my personal data is in my fireproof box.

How would I like my life celebrated or remembered?
There are many ways in which survivors can celebrate the life of their loved one. Some people prefer a memorial soon after the death; others on an anniversary marking the death. Celebrations include planting trees, creating a library fund, and establishing a foundation.

Why do we have rituals to mark the passing of a loved one? It helps the mourners to move into a spring, a renewal after grief. Many hospices have an annual event or memorial service. Attendees pack a picnic, release balloons, or add to a memorial garden. In the Jewish tradition, the one-year anniversary of the death is the date of the unveiling and installation of the grave marker.

My current preference to celebrate my life is to support organizations that are committed to the protection of otters. Otters make people smile.

If people want to contribute in my honor to a favorite charity, where do I want those contributions to go?
A school teacher in my town left a lasting legacy of books to our community. She established, in her will, a fund that buys books for children. She wanted her gradeschoolers to have an abundant supply of books. She asked that all contributions support her fund.

Many of us have a favorite charity whose purposes we support. Whether it is the American Red Cross, a church, a community fund, or a medical research organization, it is probably a good idea to let your loved ones know what organizations are most important to you. Offer people a choice of two or three organizations, so that they can contribute in accordance with their own beliefs also.

Contributions to support Honey Rock Camp, where I was exposed to spirituality as a child, would please me.

What financial arrangements need to be made for my funeral? Financial arrangements are one of the biggest burdens we can remove from our grieving loved ones. Immediately after our death, they will be asked to make decisions and pay for whatever funeral or memorial arrangements are needed. According to the American Association of Retired Persons, traditional funerals cost an average of thirty-five hundred dollars, excluding a burial plot and a marker.

You may wish to consider whether you will have made your purchasing decisions while you were alive in order to ease that burden. For example, do you want to prepay a funeral home, prepay your cremation society, buy a cemetery plot, and order a grave marker? Have you made provisions in your will to reimburse the expenses for these items? Our culture doesn't provide a clear direction as to whether the person dying should finance their own death-related affairs, or whether the family should handle the affairs out of honor for the deceased.

One of the most dramatic cultural insights I've had was in Bali, Indonesia. Although Indonesia is primarily Muslim, Bali is predominantly Hindu.

My guide, a young man in his mid-twenties, shared with me his experience. As the oldest son, his major responsibility was to save enough money to properly finance a funeral procession for his father. The complete ritual would include festivities, meals, and religious rituals. It would culminate in the dispersing of his father's ashes into the ocean. This practice can be deferred years after the person dies, until the son can afford it. It can take a young man up to three years to save the money necessary for that one event.

I believe that my funeral service is for me, as well as for my loved ones. My choices and decisions are made for my objectives. And although my loved ones will modify and shape the details to their own comfort, I think it is appropriate to self-fund this spiritual event as much as possible. My will has a provision for my funeral plans.

Do I want a visitation or a wake? Whom do I want invited? The purpose of a visitation or a wake, generally speaking, is to support the grievers and provide personal time for them to say good-bye to the deceased. A visitation or a wake is devoted more to the mourners than to the deceased. At some wakes, however, there is a liturgical service blessing the deceased and the loved ones.

In my first draft of my funeral plans, I announced that I did not want a visitation service, nor a casket. I justified this decision because most of my friends were scattered around the country and there were only a few close friends nearby. Now, I live in a different town. People have convinced me that I should have a wake because I now have many, many friends in the community who would like a private time to say good-bye. So I have chosen to provide for that need of theirs.

Do I want an open or closed casket? Some people think an open casket is maudlin. They say, "They are dead and gone; why would we want to look at a painted face?" Others argue that "seeing is believing" and that the reality of death is far more dramatic when mourners have that last chance to view the departed. Over the years, "Dear Abby" and Ann Landers and the grief literature have addressed this question. Counselors working with families after a

[margin: Wake/ Visitation]

death usually recommend an open casket, especially for the benefit of surviving children. An open casket can minimize any creative imaginations that hypothesize that the loved one who has "gone away" will return.

I haven't been to a wake or a funeral of a relative. But I have had to say final good-byes to pets. Although animals are clearly not human, a relationship with a pet can be very significant. I've had several meaningful bonds with cats and dogs. Some of my pets have died naturally; others I've had to have put to sleep. In each case, it has been important for me to see them and hold them after they have died. Through these experiences, I have a profound appreciation for open caskets, and I've chosen to have an open one for myself.

What type of service do I want conducted at my wake? Some denominations have specific wake services. Others do not. I don't request one.

Funeral/ Memorial

Where do I want my funeral or memorial service? Of course, this presumes that you want one. A funeral service generally has a religious component and occurs before a burial. A memorial service might not have a religious component and can be held before or after burial.

Funerals and memorial services may be done at a church or a funeral home. Memorials are often held in private and public places of beauty—parks, riverbanks, or family homes.

In some instances, the deceased may have a strong tie to a religion, but the family may not. If you have strong feelings about what should or should not be done for you, make your wishes known. I would like my service to be held at my church.

What flowers or other symbols/decorations would I like at my funeral or memorial service? I want *lots* of flowers! Lots of white flowers. And especially lots of white scented flowers. I love gardenias, lilies of the valley, freesias, roses. I don't want contributions "in lieu of flowers." I have made my wishes known to those who love me—I want flowers! Some people no doubt will say, "It's a waste of money; she won't know." I speculate that I *will* know.

Following my B.I.D. I developed more courage to do more crazy things. One time I took a gliding lesson over the Mojave Desert. It was so quiet. And the vistas were so clear. I've also taken a hot air balloon ride over Aspen, Colorado. In both instances I remember being stunned because, looking down, I could see so clearly. I could see jackrabbits running and fish swimming. It's just possible that although I won't be immediately in the room with those beautiful flowers, I will know that they are there.

What music would I like at my funeral or memorial service? A man from my church had been a fellow cancer sojourner. He was a businessman in the piano and organ business, and he had been a music teacher for thirty-five years. For his funeral, a Steinway grand piano was brought into our sanctuary. All of us who attended were blessed when his former students honored him with classical music. It was very touching. How much and what music we choose is a very personal decision.

I've already said that the music is important to me. I have requested the first verses of some favorite hymns: I'd like "In the Garden" and "Just a Closer Walk with Thee" for my father, "How Great Thou Art" for my mother, and "What a Friend We Have in Jesus" for me. I would love to hear the uplifting notes of Vivaldi, Telemann, and Albioni. I love Baroque trumpet, flute, and oboe sounds.

What Scripture or readings would I like at my funeral or memorial service? In my tradition you can't pick. There is a standard service, and part of that service includes the daily reading.

Since I want to personalize my own service, I am asking for a memorial service, perhaps held in the narthex prior to going into the sanctuary, for my burial rite. In this context, I may choose words of solace, a message I want to leave, or words that represent my outlook on life.

I want John 3:16-17 to be read. And Psalm 121.

Whom would I like to serve as my eulogist? The eulogist is the person who stands during the service and gives a testimony about how they remember you. Sometimes it is a son or daughter, or a best friend. Most generally it is a long-time friend. Immediate family members are often not well enough to take this responsibility. A local Methodist minister had a fellow minister friend serve as his eulogist. I was touched by the readings from the book *Cold Sassy Tree*.

In the Episcopal tradition, eulogies are not allowed during the funeral service. So if I were to want some comments made, they would need to be made near my beautiful, abundant display of flowers out in the narthex prior to my funeral service! I don't want to ask anyone to take on such a responsibility. I believe that choice should be my parents' decision.

Whom would I like to serve as my homilist? The homilist is usually the ordained member of the clergy. In churches with more than one minister, you usually may express your preference. Former or guest clergy can also preside at the funeral. However, courtesy dictates that you get prior approval from the current minister.

Rick, my priest for ten years, has recently accepted a new calling as the dean of a cathedral. We are currently being served by an interim priest. Perhaps Rick would accept an invitation.

Whom would I like to serve as my pallbearers? Pallbearers are the people, usually men, who carry the casket in the church and in the cemetery. It is a place of honor, similar to being in a bridal party. Often a grieving spouse asks someone to select the pallbearers. Churches may arrange for pallbearers, often using ushers. If you want certain people to be your pallbearers, then let your loved ones know. Here is one area where the literal time and place will shape the selection of people.

How would I like my service to be personalized? Barbara introduced herself to me after she read my first book, *When Your Friend Gets Cancer: How You Can Help*. She was instrumental in the creation of our nearby Cancer Wellness Center. We met several times and talked about survivorship and service. She died about a year and a half after we met. A popular inspirational speaker, she made presentations on attitude adjustment. She was famous in her circle for her belief in angels.

Barbara was a member of the Roman Catholic church. I was grateful to see several "personalized touches" in her service. In the Catholic service, there is a moment where everyone is asked to exchange a sign of peace, often a handshake or a kiss. During that moment in Barbara's service, her teenaged children went down the aisles and sent down each row a basket containing tiny angel pins for us to pin on our pew-mates. As a result, everyone left the service with one of Barbara's beloved angels.

In addition, as we were filing out of the church, a tape player played a recorded speech that Barbara had given at the national convention of Make Today Count. We heard her own voice bless us with her motto, "Dream It and Be It." At the door, we were handed a copy of her poem by that name, which has as its chorus,

Dream it. Be it.
You have the potential; it's right inside of you.
Our life is like a Kaleidoscope, and with each
*   turn we see*
The many facets and dimensions that we alone
*   can be.*

Given that my funeral service will use *The Book of Common Prayer*, personal tailoring would have to happen during a memorial in the narthex, prior to my funeral.

If I have a memorial service, I would like the tone to be short, simple, and clear. I would like the theme to be one of celebration and thanksgiving. I'd like everyone to know I am grateful for the Easter story of salvation and the promise of life hereafter. In addition, if anyone would inquire how I had been near the time of my death, I would like them told that I was curious and optimistic, and even at times eager, to continue my sojourn with God into another world. The most important wish that I have, however, is to acknowledge that I would like all decisions made to support my parents' grief; that I have recorded these specific funeral details, but that every one of these should be modified to accommodate my parents' desires.

What type of service do I want conducted at my funeral or memorial service? Traditions vary widely in their rituals and protocols. For instance, we Episcopalians have two burial rites in our *Book of Common Prayer*, Burial Rite I and Burial Rite II. I am leaving this decision up to my parents; the sound of the service will be more important to them than to me.

Committal **Do I want to be cremated?** Cremation has increased in popularity over the years. Generally speaking, the expenses for cremating the body are less than for preparing the body and placing it in a specially sealed casket and vault. In addition, disposing cremains in formal cemeteries requires less space and is becoming more popular with conservationists. Cremains can be disposed in more places as well.

After I was diagnosed with cancer and started to inquire about burials, I asked my minister at the time if our denomination believed that full-body burial was necessary for one to be in a proper condition for the Second Advent. I was concerned that I would not be eligible for joining Jesus and rising to the heavens if I was cremated. The minister directed me to make an appointment with a theological scholar at a university.

Based on my talk with the scholar, I understand that my progression to heaven will not be based on the disposition of my body after my death. However, I've met many men and women from different religious backgrounds who insist that I will be limiting my chances by such an action! I know one group of believers who require not only full-body burial but also above-ground burial with feet facing east.

Down deep, I knew that everlasting life is not dependent on being buried or cremated. However, when I was so sick, I didn't want to do anything other than what would be most acceptable to God. My pursuit for information was driven by a strong desire to do what God would want. And I didn't want to rely on my inexperienced and uneducated mind. So I asked many questions. In the end, I decided that I want to be cremated.

Where do I want my cremains to go? You and your loved ones have many options to consider for your cremains. Should they be scattered? Where? In a favorite place, a meadow, a church yard, the sea? Should they be buried?

When my friend Bill died, his family gathered to scatter his ashes in a most moving way. Bill and his wife, Rae, loved the prairie and were restoring part of their property back into a true "natural prairie."

His daughter, Diane, combined his ashes with wildflower seeds. Then she divided the mixture into beautifully wrapped, small packets, similar to those provided at weddings. The individually wrapped packets were placed in a beautiful basket, one packet for each member of the family. At the appointed time, they each took a packet and quietly walked into the prairie. Each in his own way, at his own pace, with his own private memories, scattered Bill's ashes. The wildflowers have taken, and return each year.

In addition to scattering cremains, there are other options. I discovered that cremains can be buried in a family plot, where they take up less space than would a casket. Some people keep the cremains of their loved ones in their home. Cremains may also be placed in a mausoleum or vault.

In Thailand, cremains are boxed and tucked away in corners of gardens. Sometimes they are housed in crypts under foundations supporting the huge reclining Buddhas. When I traveled in Borneo, I discovered marvelous and beautiful columbaria in a Chinese Buddhist temple—tall, elaborate structures placed in the most sacred part of the temples. Each columbarium contains hundreds of small vaults. Each vault is marked with a beautiful three-by-three-inch plaque naming the person within. The columbaria reminded me of the safe deposit boxes at the bank.

Christian churches often have places for cremains. I would like to have my cremains returned to a sacred place, a Christian church, and placed either in an outdoor garden wall or in a columbarium or scattered in the garden.

Do I want to be buried? For centuries around the world, families have buried their deceased—in sacred and secular cemeteries. Most people associate burial with full-body burial. However, cremains can be buried. The most common definition for burial means "to put one's body in a special place." When we think of being buried, our options are to be below ground or above ground and in a public or private place.

Some people wonder whether it is still possible to have their body for burial if they are donating organs or releasing their body for medical research or experimentation. The answer is yes. Research or experimentation may delay the burial from one week to three months, but it can be done.

Where do I want to be buried? Some people may want to be buried near their church. Others may look forward to a "pretty" location. And some may not care at all! Historically, many people have wanted to be buried and join their loved ones in an extended family plot. And that option can become more challenging— to the plot of the mother's family or the father's? In today's hodgepodge of blended families, extended families, divorced families, and nontraditional families, there are many choices.

I arranged to spend a few days in a Benedictine abbey in Arkansas. I was intrigued by one of the practices of these monks. It is important to them to have their dead brothers in their midst. This arrangement supports one of the Benedictine Rules, which reminds everyone to face death daily and "to die into each night and to be born into each day." The cemetery is in view from nearly every place on the grounds. As part of my retreat there, I walked the Stations of the Cross, which ends very symbolically at that cemetery. I saw a recent grave that was as yet unmarked. In this religious community, the brothers want to be buried in the center of the community that has sustained and nurtured them throughout their lives.

The Benedictines are not the only ones who emphasize sacred sites. I read recently that in 1993, nearly twelve hundred bodies had been shipped to Israel for burial. Two-thirds of them were nonresidents who had never lived there yet who wanted to be buried in the Holy Land.

Throughout my travels, I have noticed a great diversity in cultural customs. In small, medieval villages in Normandy and Brittany, France, the cemetery has been a place of beauty, on or near the center of town, a park that is often visited by local families for evening strolls. Fresh-cut flowers decorate graves that are over 250 years old. In fact, if you want to see some of the most modern designs for cut flower decorations, they can be found in the cemetery.

I visited my friend Barbara, who was a Peace Corps volunteer in Senegal, West Africa. I did not notice a cemetery anywhere within the village. When I inquired of the local residents where their cemetery was, I received a gesture: "Way over there down the path on the other side of the peanut fields."

In Southeast Asia, there are massive cemeteries on the mountainsides, where one can see the separate ethnic sections. It is striking to see the different traditions offset with flowers and fences and grave markers.

Nancy, a nurse, told me that, to celebrate her father's life, Nancy and her sister bought a sapling and planted it in the cemetery, near their father's grave. Her sister has since died of cancer and was buried next to her father. The tree that they had planted together had grown and provided shade for everyone at her sister's burial service.

Do I want a religious service at my cremains or burial site? Historically, burials have been on religious or church grounds. Given the design of modern churches and the need for parking lots, it is becoming more and more difficult to be buried on church property. As a result, more people are being buried in community cemeteries. Consequently, for many people a religious service at a burial site is significant and requested.

What kind of marker do I want? Shirley, a friend from college, told me that it was a difficult decision for her and her mother and sisters to decide what type of marker would be appropriate for her father's grave. She also heightened my awareness that our lives are often summarized with a few brief words on our marker. Her comments led me to wonder what my parents would want for their markers.

Although my mother and I have always shared a love of traipsing through old cemeteries and reading the markers, we hadn't discussed our own preferences. During a fall leaf-viewing trip in New England, my mother and father and I drove to Barre, Vermont, to see a famous monument manufacturing company, Rock of Ages.

Under the guise of doing research for my work, we arrived in time to take a tour of the facilities. We saw the mammoth carving rooms and the etching and finishing area. The tour ended in a display garden where the company features examples of their markers. Success! After asking which examples they liked and why, I now know their respective preferences.

You might wonder why I didn't ever ask them directly. Some things are difficult to bring up. But we should—either directly or indirectly.

If you elect to have your ashes scattered, you might consider having a marker in the vicinity of your ashes. Children and grandchildren often express their sorrow at not having a "place" to go and visit their relative or friend.

If having my cremains placed in a church garden wall or columbarium will be possible, I'm sure the church will have its rules regarding types of markers!

What do I want to be written on my marker? Today's contemporary technology permits great creativity in marking and carving—icons, logos, maps, flags, and even carved photo engravings, in addition to the more traditional name, date, and birthplace.

I searched in the dictionary for the difference between epithet and epitaph. Epithet refers to words written about a person. An epitaph consists of words written on a grave marker. Do you want an epithet on your epitaph?

When I saw Robert Frost's marker with a line from his poetry which says, "I had a lover's quarrel with the world," I realized that it does matter what's written there. Edgar Lee Masters wrote *The Spoon River Anthology* based on the information carved on the grave markers found in a central Illinois town.

You can preplan and prepay your marker, just as you can other aspects of your funeral plans. You may wish to consider this to further ease the burden on your loved ones or simply to ensure that you are remembered as you wish to be.

The questions used in this chapter appear in the Ready to Live Checklist beginning on page 141.

10

Thoughts on Afterlife

Where will you be? At the driving range trying out your seven iron? Reading the great books you never got around to? Singing "Holy, Holy, Holy" with the angels?

One of the most caring acts we can do for our loved ones is to share our thoughts on the afterlife. Anyone who has lost someone can tell you where he or she imagines a loved one is: "He's no doubt fishing." "She's finally sewing that quilt she always planned to do." "Our son is practicing his line drives to left field." "He's at choir practice, where else?" These images give us comfort.

But it isn't necessary for our loved ones to be *imagining* where we are and, for that matter, what we will be doing. Instead, we have the choice to tell others what we expect and hope for.

I met Linda at a talk I gave. During the following months, we corresponded frequently. I also visited her in two different hospitals. I saw her the week she died. To prepare her family and friends, Linda wrote a faith testimony called "My Testimony." She gave her testimony to everyone she could possibly give it to, including me. In it, she spoke of her life and her faith. To all of us who read it, she wrote, "I will live in God's kingdom forever and ever. I'll have a new body, no cancer, and that will be great." What a beautiful blessing for all of us to receive—to know that she thought she would be well forever and ever.

Linda took the time and effort to tell her loved ones something they wanted to hear. What would you like to tell your loved ones?

I want to tell my loved ones that I want to join the family of saints. I want to be Amy, the saint of the sea otters. Imagine me invisibly traveling around the world and assuring their well-being!

When I returned from the Galapagos, I marched right through this getting-ready-to-die checklist and came to a cold, dead stop. I found myself asking, What do I believe about the afterlife? I knew heaven was my destination, but I didn't know what heaven would be like. And I wanted to look forward to my next destination. The guidebooks weren't descriptive enough. I wanted to break through that great mystery.

So I pursued the runner-up option; I sought heaven on earth.

I went to New Zealand. And what a joy New Zealand is—the Cotswolds of England, the fjords of Norway, and the Alps of Switzerland all in one country. It is beautiful. You'll find there the tallest mountain south of the equator, glaciers, many boulders and rocks along the oceanside, the famous Milford Sound, waterfalls, inlets, mountains, and incredible natural beauty.

I stayed at a sheep station run by a family: a husband, a wife, two sons, and some hired hands. They had twenty sheepdogs, a hundred male sheep, and eight thousand female sheep. There were eight thousand baby lambs when I arrived—sixteen thousand-plus animals. The place was perfect.

I spent seven days mostly thinking, praying, and wondering. Specifically, I was thinking about my own circumstance. Having been so ready to die, why was I still alive? I wanted answers and guidance for what would come next. I questioned if the Lord really loved me. I questioned if there really was a heaven. I questioned if, as stated in John 3:16, there really was everlasting life. I also wanted to immerse myself into the literal metaphor of sheep, shepherds, and little lambs.

Although I arrived too late for the lambing week, there were several lambs and their mothers in special paddocks. The rancher directed me to one paddock and said, "Amy, go do your Bible study in that area. You'll find some little ones. If you go out in the morning, you might see one that's just brand new."

The first day, I went there to do my Bible study. I had been wearing a small gold cross, and it suddenly fell into the grass. I couldn't find it. I even began questioning, *Why would I lose my cross?*

With all of my questioning, wondering, and seeming lost-ness, I continued my habit of morning Bible studies and evening vespers in that paddock area. And then I had a once-in-a-lifetime experience.

One of the expectant mothers seemed, in my opinion, about to do something. But I didn't stare at her because I am a modest person. As a suburban girl I never had much experience with cats, dogs, cows, or horses. So as I saw her trot around the paddock with her tail up and something dark emerging, I thought, *Lower my eyes; be a proper guest.* And I lowered my eyes, then lifted them a little, and then all of a sudden what had been dark and brown now appeared to be shiny and black. And two little hooves and a nose were emerging. "A lamb!" I exclaimed.

Right then the rancher's old triangle rang—*clang, clang, clang!* And the ranch hand called out, "Dinner!"

I knew I should go, but *I can eat any time,* I thought to myself. "I'm not coming. I think it's a lamb. How long does this take?" I called.

I put my Bible down and waited. Nothing came forth. At my insistence, the ranch hand went for the rancher, and the rancher, like a good shepherd, came.

It was a most moving experience for me. I had a profound insight about those green pastures. Here was the shepherd, standing by. But where was the lamb? Suddenly there was a *squish, squish.* I was thinking, *Oh, Lord, I'm going to see a lamb born!* The rancher stepped over and helped the birthing, holding the wet, wiggling thing up for me to see. "What should we call him, Amy? He's a boy." Without waiting for my reply, the shepherd named him Amos.

Here is what my Amos experience meant to me. Amos was a boy. And boy lambs become lamb chops at age six months. Girl lambs become future mother sheep, trotting up and down the mountainous hills to deliver lambs for six years, and then they become mutton chops.

But Amos did not appear to shout, "Wait! I want to go back and be a girl!" He looked like he readily accepted his lot in life. I sat there in that pen in New Zealand thinking, *What difference does it make how long we live, whether six months or six years?* And all my questioning seemed to disappear as John 3:16 became a real and cherished verse forevermore. Finally I could own and claim it:

> *For God so loved the world*
> *that he gave his one and only Son,*
> *that whoever believes in him*
> *shall not perish but have eternal life.*

I could recite with passion from Psalm 23:

> *The LORD is my shepherd,*
> *I shall not be in want.*
> *He makes me lie down in green pastures, . . .*
> *He restores my soul.*
> *Even though I walk through the valley*
> *of the shadow of death,*
> *I will fear no evil,*
> *for you are with me;*
> *your rod and your staff, they comfort me.*

And I lost all doubt.

Amos just trusted the shepherd and was thankful to be alive for the time he had. Trust and thankfulness is what I learned from him. With the ambiguity in my life, I learned that I can trust and be thankful. Amos's birth symbolized a new beginning for me. I can live each day with trust that my Shepherd is near. I can be thankful, and am thankful, for each new day of life. This "The Lord is My Shepherd" retreat marked another passage as well. In addition to thinking of Jesus as my Savior, I recognized Jesus as my shepherd.

The moment Amos was born, a true and brilliant rainbow arched over the green pasture. I felt as if God had sent a private gift just for me. The rainbow was there for a short time, but during that brief moment, I made a commitment. I promised that with the life I would have, I would share this story of Amos (six months, six years, what difference does it make when we have the promise of John 3:16?), and encourage others to consider everlasting life with Jesus.

Having lost my cross in the grass, I bought a gold charm of a sheep, to represent the Lamb of God, that I still wear today.

A few weeks after I returned from New Zealand, I went to work in Brazil. There I bought a ring of semiprecious stones that has all the colors of that symbolic rainbow. I place it on my finger every day. And every day I am reminded of God's promise of everlasting life.

Questions to consider

What do I think happens to "me" at the moment of my death?

Where do I think I go after I physically die?

Have I shared my beliefs about afterlife and my where-abouts with my loved ones?

What images, stories, places, or events can I turn to for information and comfort concerning death and what comes afterwards?

11

Trip
Delayed

With cancer in my recent past and likely to reappear in the near future, I had planned accordingly. I had been so ready to die. It was as if I had picked a destination, packed my bags, hurried down the terminal corridor, looked up at the departure monitor, and saw flashing "Trip Delayed." Now what do I do? Stay put and wait? Go home and come back again? Rebook another route?

I felt like my car was in idle, and I didn't know whether to put it in reverse or to put it into drive, maybe even overdrive.

But I couldn't stay in the terminal forever. Nor could I idle away. I needed to renew my commitment to life. Here are some of the ways I found that helped me keep going.

Is He Cute? Is He Really, Really Cute? It was close to Christmas, and Chicago was glorious with decorations and twinkling lights. I said to Flannel, out loud, as some cat people would understand, "Do I bore you? Do you bore me? Isn't it true that what we need is a dog?" And, in a manner which only cat lovers could understand, Flannel concurred.

The next morning I hailed a taxi and went directly to the animal shelter, instructing the driver to wait for me and the boy dog I was about to get from inside. I entered the building with a boldness and a commitment to new but modest beginnings. My strategy was that any boy dog who would come to the front of the pen, and in his own way would "speak" to me, would come home with me.

Had I said anything out loud, the conversation would have been, "You're on death row; I'm on death row. Let's give each other some company." I figured that three months with me was better than three months where he was. But not one dog came forward. Not a boy. Not a girl. None.

The cab was still waiting. Without a dog in the back seat, I asked the driver to take me straight to a bookstore. And I went directly to the animal section and purchased the *American Kennel Club's Red Book,* full of pictures of dogs. I returned home and propped it on my bed, with Flannel on the pillow next to me.

I turned the pages slowly, absorbing the photos and descriptions on each page, and continued for several pages. Then I saw the face, and I said to Flannel, "That's him."

It was a picture of a Portuguese Water Dog, which I had never seen nor heard of until that moment.

I got on the phone and called around the entire country, looking for an available puppy. I connected with Nancy Fouts near Minneapolis, who had one available.

I asked Nancy if her dog was cute—"Is he really, really cute?" She probed to understand why I was asking, and I responded candidly. I told her that I wasn't sure how long I would have him, because I had significant cancer. I told her that I was concerned about who would take him after I was gone. And Nancy said, "Don't you worry. I'll take him back in two months, or two years, or twelve years. He's that cute."

A few years ago I was in Israel with my minister and his wife, and as a take-home present for myself, I bought a silver sculpture of Joshua and Caleb. Joshua and Caleb are found in the Old Testament. They were the two men who insisted that there was indeed a Promised Land. They left their community and searched. They were bold. And when they returned, they brought with them fruits, proof of the Promised Land.

I went to Minneapolis, returned with my new puppy, and introduced him to Flannel. I named him Joshua, after the Old Testament character, so I would have a constant reminder to get off "hold" and to be bold!

He serves as my constant reminder to simplify my lifestyle, to choose priorities, to examine what's important and what's not, to let go of the past, and to celebrate the present. And as all puppies are capable of doing, he helped me realize how important it is to love, and to love unconditionally. With his help, I've been able to change my love style . . . literally. Today it is much more important for me to say "I love you" more often to more people.

Within just a few weeks of getting Joshua, the three of us moved to Geneva, a small town west of Chicago. Here I am known and loved and am an active member of the community. Now I am four blocks from my friend Polly, and four blocks from my friend Rae. Here I've found several ways to stay connected to life.

Making Strides and Accepting Affirmation

"Making Strides" is a national theme for an American Cancer Society fundraising event. I have been the speaker for my local unit's event. The term "making strides" is also reflective of how I've lived my life. Six years have passed since I swam with Sweet William the sea lion. My family and friends surprised me with a "Thank You Lordy, Amy's Forty" birthday party.

I'm full of gratitude for how I have been affirmed in the strides I am making. People often tell me, "It's good to hear you are doing well," or "You are a great survivor," or "You have succeeded in something." I *am* well. As a guest on Gary Collins's television show, I sat with Joan Borysenko, the author of the bestseller *Minding the Body, Mending the Mind*. In the green room before the show, she affirmed my wellness and autographed a copy of her book. On TV she said, "Amy is the healthiest survivor I've ever met." It was powerful to be affirmed by a notable national figure. But I'm equally, and perhaps even more, encouraged and affirmed by the consistent stream of exquisite handmade note cards from Emma, the friend of a friend, who has befriended me.

Support Networks

Part of my wellness is due to my support networks. In giving, I receive. I remain rooted to my call to live through constant volunteering. In the past few years I have served as a spokesperson for the American Cancer Society, especially for its "I Can Cope" educational program and its one-on-one visitor program, "Can-Surmount." I am a member and advocate of the National Coalition for Cancer Survivorship and local cancer support centers, especially in Chicagoland for The Cancer Wellness Center and The Wellness House. I've been especially uplifted and supported by the board of directors and the advisory group for Joshua's Tent.

Tailor-Made Tricks

The social sciences of recovery and wellness encourage us to stimulate our wellness by offering us a number of wellness tools such as creative visualization and relaxation response. I have relied on three tricks that have yet to lose their power and helpfulness for me.

Passions. I need to satisfy my senses—I need sensual stimulation. The ultimate treat for me is a trip to a new place for a new experience. For sight and smell I love to get fresh cut flowers. Touch from a trusted individual is also very important. I'm lucky my best friend Polly is superb in her field, therapeutic touch.

Mindfulness. Under stress, anxiety, frayed nerves, when we can't get focused and we feel we are losing control, we can be mindful. When we concentrate on any object, other things competing for our attention automatically disappear. Try it for yourself and see. Here's an exercise I learned from Melva at my local hospital.

EXERCISE

Hold a wrapped peppermint candy in your hand. Stroke the wrapper between your forefinger and thumb. Twirl the candy around and just feel it in your hand. After a few minutes unwrap it and look at it. See the red twirls and the white twirls. Recognize the difference in the pattern. Count the reds and the whites. Finally, put it in your mouth.

Taste it. Try moving it around with your tongue into your cheek. Push it forward into your gums in front of your teeth. Put it back into your molar area and crunch it. Burst it. Taste it.

Fifteen minutes can go by doing this exercise. If you tried it, your blood pressure probably decreased and your breathing most likely evened. And I bet you smiled, if the candy was good!

Prayer. There are times when I simply have to take a retreat and withdraw from my daily life. Silence and meditation have been part of major religious traditions for centuries. I learned valuable lessons about silence on a Zen prayer retreat—two days of silence. I found I could embrace some of the principles of Zen practices without betraying my belief in Christ. This is also called "centering prayer," as taught by Thomas Merton.

Another time, I retreated to wake up on a New Year's morning with a group of monks in their abbey. I wanted to start the New Year as I start each day, with the line "I will try to live a simple, sincere, and serene life." On New Year's eve, I drove 350 miles through a snowstorm in order to wake up in their abbey in northern Wisconsin. The New Year started with a surprise. The monks invited me to join them at their table, to feast on filet mignon, fresh asparagus, and champagne!

And I left with this gift, a prayer that I have used for the past two years. Try it: When you inhale, inhale every breath of God's air you can. And when you exhale, exhale to empty your air as forcefully as you can.

> I breathe in God the Father *(inhale)*,
> And I breathe out frustration *(exhale)*.
>
> I breathe in Jesus Christ the Son *(inhale)*,
> And I breathe out irritation *(exhale)*.
>
> I breathe in the Holy Spirit, the Comforter
> *(inhale)*,
> And I breathe out limitation *(exhale)*.

The Three Nevers

I've shared three stories about special animals that helped me gear up to live. No matter how positive, how supported, how connected we are, there are still private times of doubt and frustration, times of questioning the can-do attitude. We are overcome by uncertainty and doubt that can cripple our ability to keep moving forward, to keep on living.

My daddy often ends his cards and notes with some lines he heard a minister say in a sermon many years ago, "Never look back; never look down; never give up." Yes, there will come a time when I won't be able to keep going physically, and I will no longer be making strides. I do know, though, it won't be from a lack of trying.

To keep ourselves going in the midst of our doubt and despair, we need to have a success story: a time when we never looked down, never looked back, and never gave up—a story we can hang on to, that we can draw on in our darkness. Each of us has one of these moments, a moment when we held on, when we overcame, when we rose higher than we thought we could.

Here is my personal story of overcoming, which helps me maintain my momentum toward life. It has become my personal keepsake, my ultimate example, my always recallable personal experience of "never looking down, never looking back, never giving up."

I was having dinner in Philadelphia with my friend Pat and her daughter Sheri, whom I hadn't seen in a long time. I had to be in Chicago early the next morning to make my "Making Strides" presentation, and had a reservation on a 7:55 P.M. flight. It was the last flight out to Chicago that night. I was torn. I wanted so much to stay with these two people I loved, yet I knew I had to catch that flight to be there in the morning.

We were thirty miles from the airport, and I had a rental car to return. The clock was ticking . . . 6:20 . . . 6:30 . . . 6:40. I finally asked Pat "How do I get to the airport from here?" I had never driven to that airport. She told me, and I got in the car to go.

Have you ever been on a road or a path you were told to follow and then began to lose confidence that it really was the right way to go? You knew you should have trusted, but you weren't sure it was right? Well,

I had that feeling and decided to stop at a gas station to check. "That's right, that's right, I-70 west, I-70 west." All of a sudden, I realized with a sinking feeling that I was crossing a bridge over the Delaware River, and I was on the wrong bridge. It was then 7:00.

At the toll booth I asked the attendant, "How do I get to the airport?" She said, "Go back and get on 6 South." I got to 6 South, and it went from four lanes to two lanes. I knew that shouldn't happen on major roads going to major airports. I was now in South Philly, with little square blocks of row houses and men sitting on one side, and women sitting on the other side on the stoops. It was then 7:15. I could see no signs of semi trucks on an interstate or any other indicators that I was near an airport, and I was thinking frantically, *Am I going to make it? Can I really still make it?*

I found a young expectant couple strolling along hand in hand, and I pulled over to ask, "Is this the way?" The man said, "Yeah, you can go this way, but it's a long way. Keep going." The road got narrower, and I was full of doubt, now growing anxious that I would miss my flight, be stranded, and fail to be present in the morning for my talk.

I came upon a policeman at a four-way stop intersection and asked, "Is this the way?" He said, "Yeah, but there's an easier way." Have you ever had someone say that to you, and you had to trust? Perhaps to switch gears, to switch treatments, to switch hope, to switch caregivers? You had to change because you had to get there.

Well, I went the way he suggested, and I was praying. I could now see semi trucks, but I was in an industrial park. There was still no expressway to the airport. Then I found the interstate, but it was still eleven miles from the airport, it was 7:20, and my flight was at 7:55. I pushed the speed limit of 65 m.p.h. and whipped into the rent-a-car place. Then I was kicking myself—Why hadn't I put this car on a credit card in the first place? Now I had to wait because I was paying by check. And with nine minutes to go to get to my gate, the agent was dialing up some computer somewhere to see if my check would bounce!

I asked, "How often do these little jitney buses get here to take us to the airport?" He gave me a vague answer. But lo and behold, an angel appeared. He said to me, "I'll get you a driver." Have you ever been so low that you didn't know how you could do it, and then someone from out of the blue took pity on you? Well, a driver drove me in a private car—right up to the door. United was going to depart right on time. It was a Friday night. There were three minutes to go, and I said to the lady behind the desk, "Can I get the 7:55 to Chicago?" She said, "You have two minutes, and it's Gate D-6 . . . Run!"

I was thinking, *I have a rebuilt bum leg, and I have one lung now. I can't run!* But I kept on trying, because I wasn't going to quit. I was going to try to be there. I glanced up at the monitor and saw clearly that I had two minutes, and I saw this little cart coming. You know the kind—they zip through the airport going *"beep beep beep beep,* passengers coming!" I was running, and I saw this cart, and I asked, "Driver, will you take me to D-6?" and he said, "Sorry, another airline only." I was huffing and puffing, I had one minute to go, and I heard suddenly, "Wait a minute, we'll take you!" Someone had told that driver to help me. I got to the gate at 7:55, and two ladies said, "Sorry, the gate is closed." I was only fifteen seconds late, but the gate was closed.

Well, God makes miracles. A man said, "Wait." They brought the plane back. "Do you have your ticket?" We ran down the ramp together, and he was pulling my ticket as we ran. I made it on the plane, even though it was not of my own doing.

The importance of this story is *trying*—just trying and not quitting—trying, and along the way finding the help we need. We may run into barriers taller than a building—barriers as big as AIDS or cancer or degenerative diseases—but if we keep trying, and if we overcome our inner voice of doubt and despair, somehow there will always be people there to help us when we least expect it.

I know that I am not responsible for how long I will live—for how many days my life will have. But I am responsible to never give up, to try to do what I need to do. There are always intervening doubts and insecurities: *I'm lost; I can't find my way; the door is closed; the way has run out.* But we can't lose sight of our commitment to live. If we struggle, if we rise above our fears and doubts, then the help and support we need will always be there to guide us on our way.

Never look back; never look down; never give up.

12

Prepared to Die,
Ready to Live!

As ready as I am to go, the Lord has yet to take my soul.

At the most recent National Coalition for Cancer Survivorship's national convention, Judi Johnson, the author of the classic *I Can Cope,* asked us to select one word to describe ourselves. We went around the room disclosing our words. Sitting in a circle, I listened to the words called out.

More words were approaching me around the circle. They included "I am determined," "I am caring," "I am funny." When it was my turn I said, "I am joy." I surprised myself with that response, because I am not my image of the word *joy.* I don't look like a joy. I don't act like a joy. I don't sound like a joy.

With reflection, I know exactly from where that insight came. I remember buying a JOY! banner to hang outside my house one Christmas holiday. In the same week I hung the banner, I received a Christmas card that gave the acronym for the word *JOY: J* stands for *Jesus* first, *O* stands for *others* second, and *Y* stands for *yourself* last. I am joy in that I start my day in prayer, putting Jesus first.

I'm not comfortable with trying to describe an intimacy with Jesus. But I do want to convey a deeply held trust in him. I live my life with the deepest faith that "Even though I walk through the valley of the shadow of death, I will fear no evil, for you are with me; your rod and your staff, they comfort me."

When it comes to others, I try to follow our Sunday benediction: "Go in peace to love and serve the Lord."

And now I'm fortunate, with a great blessing. My dream has come true. Under the auspices of Joshua's Tent, a not-for-profit organization, I am now able to do talks, workshops, and retreats for patients and professionals, for everyone, on the themes I've covered in this book.

I am glad there's a *Y* in the word joy—*Y* for *yourself.* Remember Joshua? I asked if he was really, really cute because I wanted him to be able to find a home? I haven't had to return him. He's been a constant companion. I've cherished his love and had a dream to let someone else experience a Joshua. I thought how wonderful he would be in an AIDS hospice lounge greeting families and friends; how wonderful he would be on the dining room porch of a kids' cancer camp, greeting campers at the door.

What could be a better vision than the son of Joshua in these settings? Judy and Bruce Meiloch, handlers and breeders of Portuguese Water Dogs, asked to use Joshua as a stud, giving me the "pick of the litter." I accepted with great delight, intending to place Joshua's son permanently with a hospice, halfway home, or camp.

I waited excitedly through the pregnancy, and started to search for a placement home for the puppy.

I failed in my sales and marketing efforts. Hospice has OSHA regulations; halfway homes have turnover in management positions; and camp directors already have their family pets. Not only had my departure been delayed, but the son of Joshua had no future either. Unexpectedly, he's ours.

You've heard the considerable thought I used to name Joshua. Similarly, I felt the same need to find an appropriate name for the puppy. I checked out books of names from the library, looking for a name that was highly symbolic for me, or a name from the Bible. Not finding a suitable name in the books, I changed my process.

I thought through searching for the one message I needed to have constantly in front of me, underfoot. When I obtained Joshua, I needed the icon of "be bold" for a then-difficult journey. Joshua's name was from the Old Testament. At the time Joshua was used for a stud, I found myself reviewing more and more frequently Matthew 6:25-26. I was turning to the New Testament where God says, in essence, "If I feed the birds and clothe the lilies of the field, won't I care as much for you?" In Matthew 6:31 I read, "So do not worry."

When it was time for this puppy to join us, it was easy to discern what message he brought to Joshua and me. His formal name is Emmeran's Bundle of Joy. But clearly his message line reads, "Don't worry." I call him Matthew.

If you wonder how I am, you can think of me in the morning, not only seeing my symbols scattered about, but being greeted by two marvelous faces and exuberant wagging tails. When I see Joshua I remember, *Be bold! You are prepared to die.* And when I look at Matthew, I am reminded, *Don't worry, you are ready to live!*

Bibliography

The following are some books I've read and films I've watched while on my journey. Some are pieces that informed my beliefs. Others I read to become better informed. Although I do not agree with all of them, all were used along my way.

Agee, James. *A Death in the Family*. New York: Bantam Books, 1985.

Attlee, Rosemary. *William's Story*. Wheaton, Ill.: Harold Shaw Publishers, 1983.

Baden, Michael M., M.D., with Judith Adler Hennessee. *Unnatural Death: Confessions of a Medical Examiner*. New York: Random House, 1989.

Barbo, Beverly. *The Walking Wounded*. Lindsborg, Kans.: Carlsons', 1987.

Barclay, Ian. *Death and the Life to Come: What Happens When I Die?* London: Hodder and Stoughton, 1988.

Bayly, Joseph. *The Last Thing We Talk About*. Elgin, Ill.: David C. Cook Publishing Co., 1973.

Beagle, Peter S. *A Fine & Private Place*. New York: A Roc Book, Penguin Books, 1992.

Beckett, Samuel. *Waiting for Godot*. New York: Grove Press, 1954.

Beisser, Arnold, M.D. *A Graceful Passage: Notes on the Freedom to Live or Die*. New York: Bantam Books, 1991.

Bertman, Sandra L., Ph.D. *Facing Death: Images, Insights, and Interventions*. Bristol, Penn.: Taylor & Francis Publishers, 1991.

Bieber, Connie. *The Lord Is My Shepherd*. Elgin, Ill.: David C. Cook Publishing Co., 1991.

Borysenko, Joan, Ph.D. *Fire in the Soul: A New Psychology of Spiritual Optimism*. New York: Warner Books, 1993.

Borysenko, Joan, Ph.D. *Minding the Body, Mending the Mind*. New York: Bantam Books, 1988.

Boulden, Jim. *Life & Death: A Collected Wisdom*. Santa Rosa, Calif.: Desktop published, 1989.

Boulden, Jim. *Saying Goodbye: Coloring Book for Grieving Children*. Santa Rosa, Calif.: Desktop published, 1989.

Broyard, Anatole. *Intoxicated by My Illness: And Other Writings on Life and Death*. New York: Clarkson Potter, Publishers, 1992.

Burnham, Betsy. *When Your Friend Is Dying*. Grand Rapids, Mich.: Chosen Books, Zondervan Corporation, 1982.

Burnham, Sophy. *A Book of Angels*. New York: Ballantine Books, 1990.

Burnham, Sophy. *Angel Letters*. New York: Ballantine Books, 1991.

Burns, Olive Ann. *Cold Sassy Tree*. New York: Dell Publishing, 1984.

Buscaglia, Leo, Ph.D. *The Fall of Freddie the Leaf: A Story of Life for All Ages*. Thorofare, N.J.: Slack, Incorporated, 1982.

Callanan, Maggie, and Patricia Kelley. *Final Gifts: Understanding the Special Awareness, Needs, and Communications of the Dying*. New York: Poseidon Press/Simon & Schuster, Inc., 1992.

Carver, Raymond. *A New Path to the Waterfall*. New York: The Atlantic Monthly Press, 1989.

Cather, Willa. *Death Comes for the Archbishop*. New York: Random House, Vintage Books Edition, 1971.

Coetzee, J. M. *Age of Iron*. New York: Random House, 1990.

Concerning Death: A Practical Guide for the Living. Edited by Earl A. Grollman. Boston: Beacon Press, 1974.

Cox, Elizabeth. *Thanksgiving: An AIDS Journal*. New York: Harper & Row, Publishers, Inc., 1990.

Craven, Margaret. *I Heard the Owl Call My Name*. New York: Dell Publishing, 1973.

Crichton, Michael. *The Terminal Man*. New York: Ballantine Books, 1972.

Cross, David, and Robert Bent. *Dead Ends: An Irreverent Field Guide to the Graves of the Famous*. New York: A Plume Book, Penguin Books, 1991.

De Mello, Anthony. *The Song of the Bird*. New York: Doubleday, 1984.

De Mello, Anthony. *Sadhana A Way to God: Christian Exercises In Eastern Form*. New York: Doubleday, 1984.

De Mello, Anthony. *Wellsprings: A Book of Spiritual Exercises*. New York: Doubleday, 1986.

De Caussade, Jean-Pierre. *The Sacrament of the Present Moment*. New York: Harper & Row, 1982.

Deciding to Forego Life-Sustaining Treatment. Washington, D.C.: President's Commission for the Study of Ethical Problems in Medicine and Biomedical and Behavioral Research, March, 1983.

DeGrandis, Rev. Robert, S.S.J. *The Stations of the Cross*. Printed in the U.S. by the author, 1983.

Dobihal, Edward F., Jr., and Charles William Stewart. *When a Friend is Dying: A Guide to Caring for the Terminally Ill and Bereaved*. Nashville, Tenn.: Abingdon Press, 1984.

Dossey, Larry, M.D. *Healing Words: The Power of Prayer and the Practice of Medicine*. New York: HarperCollins Publishers, 1993.

Duda, Deborah. *Coming Home: A Guide to Dying at Home with Dignity*. New York: Aurora Press, 1987.

DuFresne, Florine. *Home Care: An Alternative to the Nursing Home*. Elgin, Ill.: The Brethren Press, 1985.

Eadie, Betty J., with Curtis Taylor. *Embraced by the Light*. Placerville, Calif.: Gold Leaf Press, 1992.

Edgerton, Clyde. *In Memory of Junior*. Chapel Hill, N.C.: Algonquin Books, 1992.

Farnsworth, Ken. *The Ultimate Healing*. Wilton, Conn.: Morehouse Publishing, 1989.

Feinstein, David, and Peg Elliott Mayo. *Rituals for Living & Dying*. San Francisco: Harper San Francisco, 1990.

Forbes, Malcolm, with Jeff Bloch. *They Went That-A-Way*. New York, Simon & Schuster, 1988.

Friend, David, and the Editors of *Life*. *The Meaning of Life: Reflections in Words and Pictures on Why We Are Here.* Boston: Little, Brown and Company, 1991.

Friend, David, and the Editors of *Life*. *More Reflections on the Meaning of Life.* Boston: Little, Brown and Company, 1992.

Gaebelein, A. C. *What the Bible Says about Angels.* Grand Rapids, Mich.: Baker Book House, 1988.

Graham, Billy. *Facing Death and the Life After.* Waco, Tex.: Word Books, 1987.

Greene, Bob, and D. G. Fulford. *To Our Children's Children: Preserving Family Histories for Generations to Come.* New York: Doubleday, 1992.

Grof, Stanislav and Christina. *Beyond Death: The Gates of Consciousness.* New York: Thames and Hudson Inc., 1980.

Grollman, Earl A. *Living When a Loved One Has Died.* Boston: Beacon Press, 1987.

Hammerschlag, Carl A., M.D. *The Dancing Healers: A Doctor's Journey of Healing with Native Americans.* San Francisco: Harper & Row, 1988.

Harper, George Lea, Jr. *Living with Dying: Finding Meaning in Chronic Illness.* Grand Rapids, Mich.: William B. Eerdmans Publishing Company, 1992.

Harwell, Amy. *When Your Friend Gets Cancer: How You Can Help.* Wheaton, Ill.: Harold Shaw Publishers, 1987.

Hayes, Helen. *A Gathering of Hope.* Garden City, N.Y.: Doubleday, 1985.

Hill, T. Patrick, and David Shirley. *A Good Death: Taking More Control at the End of Your Life.* New York: Addison-Wesley Publishing Company, Inc., 1992.

Hoffman, Dona. *Yes, Lord.* St. Louis: Concordia Publishing House, 1975.

Holden, Edith. *The Nature Notes of An Edwardian Lady.* New York: Arcade Publishing, a division of Little Brown, 1989.

Holdren, Shirley, and Susan Holdren, with Candace E. Hartzler. *Why God Gave Me Pain.* Chicago: Loyola University Press, 1984.

Humphrey, Derek. *Let Me Die Before I Wake.* Los Angeles: The Hemlock Society, 1984.

Humphrey, Derek. *Final Exit*. Eugene, Oreg.: The Hemlock Society, 1991.

Huron, Rod. *Say Hello to Life: What the Bible Says about Life After Death*. Cincinnati, Ohio: The Standard Publishing Co., 1984.

Ilefeldt, W. G. *Thoughts While Tending Sheep*. New York: Crown Publishers, 1988.

Institutional Ethics Committees and Health Care Decision Making. Edited by Ronald E. Cranford, M.D., and A. Edward Doudera, J.D. Ann Arbor, Mich.: Health Administration Press, 1984.

Ireland, Jill. *Life Wish*. Boston: Little, Brown and Company, 1987.

Ivan, Leslie, and Maureen Melrose. *The Way We Die*. Chichester, West Sussex: Angel Press, 1986.

Johnson, Spencer, M.D. *The Precious Present*. New York: Doubleday, 1984.

Johnson, Judi, and Linda Klein. *I Can Cope: Staying Healthy with Cancer*. Minneapolis, Minn.: The Wellness Series from DCI Publishing, 1988.

Julian of Norwich. *A Lesson of Love: The Revelations of Julian of Norwich*. Edited and translated for devotional use by Father John-Julian, O.J.N. New York: Walker and Company, 1988.

Kelsey, Morton. *Resurrection: Release from Oppression*. New York: Paulist Press, 1985.

Kelsey, Morton T. *Afterlife: The Other Side of Dying*. New York: Crossroad, 1988.

Knott, J. Eugene, Mary C. Ribar, Betty M. Duson, and Marc R. King. *Thanatopics: Activities and Exercises for Confronting Death*. Lexington, Mass.: Lexington Books, D.C. Heath and Company, 1989.

Kopp, Ruth, M.D., with Stephen Sorenson. *When Someone You Love Is Dying*. Grand Rapids, Mich.: Ministry Resources Library, Zondervan Publishing House, 1980.

Kramer, Kenneth. *The Sacred Art of Dying: How World Religions Understand Death*. New York: Paulist Press, 1988.

Kubler-Ross, Elisabeth. *Death: The Final State of Growth*. New York: Simon & Schuster, Inc., 1986.

Kushner, Harold S. *When Bad Things Happen to Good People*. New York: Avon Books, 1983.

Langley, Myrtle. *Religions: A Book of Beliefs*. Elgin, Ill.: David C. Cook Publishing Co., 1981.

Leimbach, Marti. *Dying Young*. New York: Doubleday, 1990.

LeShan, Lawrence, Ph.D. *Cancer As a Turning Point*. New York: E. P. Dutton, 1989.

Levine, Howard. *Life Choices: Confronting the Life and Death Decisions Created by Modern Medicine*. New York: Simon & Schuster, 1986.

Levine, Stephen. *Healing into Life and Death*. Garden City, N.Y.: Anchor Press/Doubleday, 1987.

Lewis, C. S. *A Grief Observed*. New York: Walker and Company, 1985.

Linn, Mary Jane, Dennis Linn, and Matthew Linn. *Healing the Dying*. New York: Paulist Press, 1979.

Lively, Penelope. *Moon Tiger*. New York: Grove Press, 1987.

Lohmann, Jeanne. *Gathering a Life: A Journal of Recovery*. Santa Barbara, Calif.: John Daniel & Company, 1989.

Lorde, Audre. *The Cancer Journals*. San Francisco: Spinsters/Aunt Lute, 1980.

Lynch, Dorothea, and Eugene Richards. *Exploding Into Life*. New York: Aperture, with Many Voices Press, 1986.

Magee, David S. *Everything Your Heirs Need To Know: Your Assets, Family History and Final Wishes*. Chicago, Ill.: Dearborn Financial Publishing, Inc., 1991.

Maier, Frank, with Ginny Maier. *Sweet Reprieve*. New York: Crow Publishers, Inc., 1991.

Making Choices: Ethics Issues for Health Care Professionals. Edited by Emily Friedman. Chicago: American Hospital Publishing, Inc., 1986.

Malcolm, Andrew H. *Someday*. New York: Alfred A. Knopf, 1991.

Malz, Betty. *Heaven: A Bright & Glorious Place*. Old Tappen, N.J.: A Chosen Book by Fleming H. Revell Company, 1989.

Manning, Doug. *Comforting Those Who Grieve: A Guide for Helping Others*. San Francisco: Harper & Row, 1987.

Manning, Doug. *Don't Take My Grief Away: What to Do When You Lose a Loved One*. San Francisco: Harper & Row, 1984.

Masters, Edgar Lee. *Spoon River Anthology*. New York: Collier Books, Macmillan Publishing Company, 1962.

Miller, Arthur. *Death of a Salesman*. New York: Penguin Books, 1976.

Moody, Raymond A., Jr., M.D. *Life after Life*. New York: Bantam Books, 1976.

Morrow, Ed. *The Grim Reaper's Book of Days: A Cautionary Record of Famous, Infamous and Unconventional Exits*. New York: Carol Publishing Group, 1992.

Morse, Melvin, M.D. *Transformed by the Light*. New York: Villard Books, 1992.

Moyers, Bill. *Healing the Mind*. New York: Doubleday, 1993.

Mullan, Fitzhugh, M.D. *Vital Signs: A Young Doctor's Struggle with Cancer*. New York: Dell Publishing Co., 1983.

Myers, Edward. *When Parents Die: A Guide for Adults*. New York: Penguin Books, 1987.

Nessim, Susan, and Judith Ellis. *Cancervive: The Challenge of Life After Cancer*. Boston: Houghton Mifflin Company, 1991.

Nielson, Kathleen V. *No One Prepared Me for This*. Salt Lake City, Utah: Intermountain Health Care Home Health Agency, 1989.

Nouwen, Henry J. M. *A Letter of Consolation*. San Francisco: Harper & Row, 1982.

Nuland, Sherwin B. *How We Die: Reflections on Life's Final Chapter*. New York: Alfred A. Knopf, Inc., 1993.

Nungesser, Lon G., with William D. Bullock. *Notes on Living Until We Say Goodbye: A Personal Guide*. New York: St. Martin's Press, 1988.

Ogilvie, Lloyd. *12 Steps to Living without Fear*. Waco, Tex.: Word Books, 1987.

Outerbridge, David E., and Alan R. Hersh, M.D. *Easing the Passage*. New York: Harper Collins Publishers, 1991.

Owen, Howard. *Littlejohn*. New York: Villard Books, 1993.

Oxford Book of Death, The. Edited by D. J. Enright. New York: Oxford University Press, 1990.

Palmer, Greg. *Death: The Trip of a Lifetime*. New York: Harper Collins, 1993.

Park Ridge Center for the Study of Health, Faith & Ethics. *Active Euthanasia: Religion and the Public Debate*.

Peck, M. Scott, M.D. *A Bed by the Window: A Novel of Mystery and Redemption*. New York: Bantam Books, 1990.

Plath, Sylvia. *The Bell Jar*. New York: Bantam Books, 1972.

Radey, Charles, M.D. *Choosing Wisely: How Patients and Their Families Can Make the Right Decisions about Life and Death*. New York: Image Books/Doubleday, 1992.

Radner, Gilda. *It's Always Something*. New York: Simon & Schuster, 1989.

Rinpoche, Guru, according to Karma Lingpa. *The Tibetan Book of the Dead*. Translated with commentary by Francesca Fremantle & Chogyam Trungpa. Boston: Shambhala, 1987.

Rinpoche, Sogyal. *The Tibetan Book of the Living and Dying*. New York: HarperCollins, 1992.

Rollin, Betty. *Last Wish*. New York: Linden Press/Simon & Schuster, 1985.

Rupp, Joyce, O.S.M. *Praying Our Goodbyes*. Notre Dame, Ind.: Ave Maria Press, 1988.

Sanders, J. Oswald. *Heaven—Better By Far, Answers to Questions about the Believer's Final Hope*. Grand Rapids, Mich.: Discovery House Publishers, 1993.

Sarton, May. *Among the Usual Days—A Portrait*. New York: W. W. Norton & Company, 1993.

Sarton, May. *Endgame: A Journal of the Seventy-Ninth Year*. New York: W. W. Norton & Company, 1992.

Sarton, May. *Recovering: A Journal*. New York: W. W. Norton & Company, 1986.

Savage, Terry. *New Money Strategies for the '90's*. New York: HarperCollins Publishers, Inc., 1993.

Schneider, Miriam, R.N., B.S.N., and Jan Selliken Bernard, R.N., B.S.N. *Midwives to the Dying*. Sherwood, Oreg.: 1993.

Schreiber, Le Anne. *Midstream*. New York: Viking Penguin, 1990.

Selzer, Richard. *Raising the Dead: A Doctor's Encounter with His Own Mortality*. New York: Whittle Books, 1994.

Shaw, Luci. *God in the Dark*. Grand Rapids, Mich.: Broadmoor Books, Zondervan Publishing House, 1989.

Shushan, E. R., compiler. *Grave Matters*. New York: Ballantine Books, 1990.

Sibley, Brian. *C. S. Lewis: Through the Shadowlands*. Old Tappan, N.J.: Fleming H. Revell Company, 1985.

Siegel, Bernie S., M.D. *Love, Medicine & Miracles*. New York: Harper & Row Publishers, 1986.

Siegel, Bernie S., M.D. *Peace, Love & Healing*. New York: Harper & Row Publishers, 1989.

Silverman, Stephen M. *Where There's a Will . . . Who Inherited What and Why*. New York: HarperCollins Publishers, 1991.

Smalley, Gary, and John Trent, Ph.D. *The Blessing*. Nashville, Tenn.: Thomas Nelson Publishers, 1986.

Smedes, Lewis B. *Forgive and Forget: Healing the Hurts We Don't Deserve*. New York: Harper & Row, 1984.

Smolen, Rick, Phillip Moffitt, and Matthew Naythons, M.D. *The Power to Heal: Ancient Arts & Modern Medicine*. New York: Prentice Hall Press, 1990.

Soiffer, Bill. *Life in the Shadow: Living with Cancer*. San Francisco: Chronicle Books, 1991.

Sontag, Susan. *Illness as Metaphor and AIDS and Its Metaphors*. New York: Doubleday, 1990.

Spiegel, David, M.D. *Living Beyond Limits: New Hope and Help for Facing Life Threatening Illness*. New York: Times Books, Random House, 1993.

Stasey, Bobbie. *Running with the Angels: The Gifts of AIDS*. Albuquerque, N.M.: Wlysian Hills Publishing Company, 1994.

Stickney, Doris. *Water Bugs and Dragonflies*. New York: The Pilgrim Press, 1982.

Sublette, Kathleen, and Martin Flagg. *Final Celebrations: A Guide for Personal and Family Funeral Planning*. Ventura, Calif.: Pathfinder Publishing of California, 1992.

Tada, Joni Eareckson. *When Is It Right To Die? Suicide, Euthanasia, Suffering, Mercy*. Grand Rapids, Mich.: Zondervan Publishing House, 1992.

Tatelbaum, Judy. *The Courage to Grieve: Creative Living, Recovery, & Growth Through Grief*. New York: Harper & Row, 1984.

Taylor, Nick. *A Necessary End*. New York: Nan A. Talese/ Doubleday, 1992.

Thompson, Mervin E. *When Death Touches Your Life: Practical Help in Preparing for Death.* New York: Walker and Company, 1987.

Tolstoy, Leo. *The Death of Ivan Ilyich.* Translated by Lynn Solotaroff. New York: Bantam Books, 1981.

Toolan, David. *Facing West from California's Shores: A Jesuit's Journey into New Age Consciousness.* New York: Crossroad, 1987.

Toon, Peter. *Longing for Heaven: A Devotional Look at the Life after Death.* New York: Macmillan Publishing Company, 1989.

Tukankhamun: His Tomb and Its Treasures. New York: The Metropolitan Museum of Art and Alfred A. Knopf, Inc., 1976.

Vaux, Kenneth L. *Health and Medicine in the Reformed Tradition.* New York: Crossroad, 1984.

Watson, David. *Fear No Evil.* Wheaton, Ill.: Harold Shaw Publishers, 1985.

Westberg, Granger E. *Good Grief.* Philadelphia: Fortress Press, 1971.

Wiersbe, Warren W. *Why Us? When Bad Things Happen to God's People.* Old Tappan, N.J.: Power Books, 1984.

Wiesel, Elie. *Night.* Bantam Books, 1982.

Wilder, Thornton. *Our Town.* New York: Harper & Row, Perennial Edition, 1985.

Williams, Terry Tempest. *Refuge: An Unnatural History of Family and Place.* New York: Vintage Books, 1991.

Yancey, Philip. *Disappointment with God.* New York: Harper Paperbacks, 1988.

All Dogs Go To Heaven
Beaches
Citizen Kane
Cold Sassy Tree
Dad
Defending Your Life
The Dresser
An Early Frost
Ghost
The Ghost and Mrs. Muir
Ghost Dad
Flatliners
The Funeral
Harold and Maude
The King and I
King Lear
Lorenzo's Oil
Night, Mother
On Golden Pond
Out of Africa
Passed Away
Philadelphia
Shadowlands
Steel Magnolias
Terms of Endearment
Topper Returns
The Trip to Bountiful
Whose Life Is It Anyway?
Wings

**Popular
Films on
Death and
Dying**

Ready to Live Checklist

This checklist is for you to use. Feel free to remove these pages if you wish.

☐ What heroic efforts do I want?
  (e.g., none, cardiac resuscitation, respiratory support, artificial sustenance and hydration)

_____
_____
_____
_____
                    DATE

☐ Under what conditions do I wish heroic efforts withheld or withdrawn?
  (e.g., coma, persistent vegetative state)

_____
_____
_____
_____
                    DATE

☐ Are there preparatory actions I should take?

_____
_____
_____
                    DATE

Heroic Efforts and the Suicide Question

☐ What are my feelings about "self-deliverance" and "assisted suicide"?

_____

_____

_____

_____
DATE

☐ Have I talked with loved ones about my feelings and wishes concerning heroic efforts and self-deliverance?

_____

_____

_____

_____
DATE

Advance Directives

☐ Do I want to sign a living will?

_____

_____

_____

_____
DATE

☐ Is my living will signed and witnessed?

_____

_____

_____
DATE

☐ Who should have a copy of my living will in their possession?
(e.g., lawyer, family members, certain friends, clergy)

_____

_____

_____

_____
DATE

☐ Whom do I want to be involved in difficult health care decisions about my care and life support if I am incapable?
(e.g., physician, lawyer, family member, friend)

_____

_____

_____
DATE

☐ Do I want to sign a durable power of attorney for health care (DPA/HC)?

_____

_____

_____
DATE

☐ Do my key family members understand and accept my choices for my designated primary and alternate agent(s)/attorney(s) for my DPA/HC?

_____

_____

_____
DATE

☐ Who should have a copy of my durable power of attorney for health care in their possession?
(e.g., clergy, lawyer, friend, family member, physician)

_____

_____

_____
DATE

☐ Do I want to sign a durable power of attorney for property (DPA/P)?

_____

_____

_____
DATE

☐ Do my key family members understand and accept my choices for my designated primary and alternate agent(s)/attorney(s) for my DPA/P?

_____

_____

_____

_____
DATE

☐ Who should have a copy of my durable power of attorney for property in their possession?
(e.g., clergy, lawyer, friend, family member, physician)

_____

_____

_____

_____
DATE

Instruc-tions

☐ Do I want to donate organs or body parts for transplantation?

_____

_____

_____
DATE

☐ Have I signed my driver's license or organ donor card and had it witnessed?

_____

_____

_____
DATE

☐ Have I discussed my organ donation decisions with all of my loved ones?

_____

_____

_____
DATE

☐ Do I want my body used for research or experimentation?

_____

_____

_____
DATE

☐ Have all guardianship issues been resolved?
(e.g., minors, elders, pets)

_____

_____

_____
DATE

☐ Do I want to do formal estate planning?

_____

_____

_____
DATE

☐ Would estate planning minimize taxes and maximize the inheritance for my loved ones?

_____

_____

_____
DATE

☐ Do I have a Last Will and Testament?

_____

_____

_____
DATE

☐ Is my will up-to-date?

_____

_____

_____
DATE

☐ Have I provided key individuals with a copy of
my will so they will not need to access my safe
deposit box to find it?

_____

_____

_____

_____

_____
                            DATE

☐ Where do I have all of my important papers?
*(e.g., personal data: medical records—living will, durable
power of attorney for health care, donor card; legal papers—
durable power of attorney for property, guardianship directives; insurance policies, financial records and papers,
household warranties and instructions, important property
and business papers)*

_____

_____

_____

_____

_____
                            DATE

☐ Are my papers secure and in a fireproof place?

_____

_____

_____
                            DATE

☐ Do my loved ones know where to find my important papers without me?

_____

_____

_____
                            DATE

☐ What strains and tensions do I expect to surface in my dying process?
(e.g., fears, regrets, frustrations)

Strains and Tensions

_____

_____

_____

_____ DATE _____

☐ What "unfinished business" do I want to finish before I die?
(e.g., complete a project, witness a family milestone)

_____

_____

_____

_____ DATE _____

☐ To whom do I want to say good-bye?

Good-byes, Forgiveness, and Blessings

_____

_____

_____ DATE _____

☐ How do I want to say good-bye?

_____

_____

_____ DATE _____

☐ What am I doing to prepare my loved ones for their grief work when I am gone?
(e.g., tailor-made "gifts of love," personal letters, journals, photo albums, scrapbooks, videotapes)

_____

_____

_____ DATE _____

☐ What forgiveness do I want to give?

_____

_____

_____
DATE

☐ What forgiveness do I want to receive?

_____

_____

_____
DATE

☐ What blessings do I want to give?

_____

_____

_____
DATE

☐ What blessings do I want to receive?

_____

_____

_____
DATE

Final Moments
☐ What do I expect to happen to me—physically, emotionally, and spiritually—during my final moments?

_____

_____

_____
DATE

☐ Whom do I want with me when I die?

_____

_____

_____
DATE

☐ Whom don't I want with me when I die?

_____

_____

_____

_____
                        DATE

☐ Where do I want to be—home, hospital, nursing home, hospice?

_____

_____

_____

_____
                        DATE

☐ What "rites of transition" do I want as I am dying?
(e.g., prayers, songs, religious rituals)

_____

_____

_____

_____
                        DATE

☐ Whom do I want to be notified of my death?   **Funerals**

_____

_____

_____

_____
                        DATE

☐ Have I prepared a list so that my survivors can do this easily?

_____

_____

_____
                        DATE

☐ What type of announcement or notification
would I like sent to people?

_____

_____

_____

_____
                              DATE

☐ Have I discussed this announcement with my
loved ones?

_____

_____

_____

_____
                              DATE

☐ Is there a special outfit I want to be buried in?

_____

_____

_____

_____
                              DATE

☐ What do I want to have with me in my casket, if
I have one?

_____

_____

_____
                              DATE

☐ Are the details necessary for my obituary readily
available?
*(e.g., birth certificate, names and addresses of family mem-
bers, important biographical facts, military records)*

_____

_____

_____
                              DATE

☐ How would I like my life celebrated or remembered?

(e.g., plant a tree, make a donation, build a memorial, release balloons)

_____

_____

_____

_____
DATE

☐ If people want to contribute in my honor to a favorite charity, where do I want those contributions to go?

_____

_____

_____

_____
DATE

☐ What financial arrangements need to be made for my funeral?

_____

_____

_____

_____
DATE

☐ Do I want a visitation or a wake?

_____

_____
DATE

Wake/ Visitation

☐ Whom do I want invited?

_____

_____

_____
DATE

☐ Do I want an open or closed casket?

_____

_____
DATE

☐ What type of service do I want conducted at my
wake?

_____

_____

_____
DATE

Funeral/
Memorial

☐ Where do I want my funeral/memorial service?

_____

_____
DATE

☐ What flowers or other symbols/decorations
would I like at my funeral/memorial service?

_____

_____

_____
DATE

☐ What music would I like at my funeral/memo-
rial service?

_____

_____

_____
DATE

☐ What Scripture or readings would I like at my fu-
neral/memorial service?

_____

_____

_____
DATE

☐ Whom would I like to serve as my eulogist?

_____

_____

_____
DATE

☐ Whom would I like to serve as my homilist?

_____

_____

_____
DATE

☐ Whom would I like to serve as my pallbearers?

_____

_____

_____
DATE

☐ How would I like my service to be personalized?

_____

_____

_____

_____
DATE

☐ What type of service do I want conducted at my funeral or memorial service?

_____

_____

_____

_____
DATE

☐ Do I want to be cremated?   **Committal**

_____

_____

_____
DATE

☐ **Where do I want my cremains to go?**
(e.g., scattered in a favorite place or churchyard; buried in a cemetery; in a columbarium, mausoleum, or my home)

_____

_____

_____

_____
DATE

☐ **Do I want to be buried?**
(e.g., above ground, below ground, cemetery, church yard)

_____

_____

_____

_____
DATE

☐ **Where do I want to be buried?**
(e.g., family plot, childhood home, another country)

_____

_____

_____

_____
DATE

☐ **Do I want a religious service at my cremains or burial site?**

_____

_____

_____

_____
DATE

☐ **What kind of marker do I want?**

_____

_____

_____
DATE

☐ What do I want to be written on my marker?
(e.g., epitaph, important dates, epithet, maiden and married names)

_____

_____

_____

_____
DATE

☐ What do I think happens to "me" at the moment of my death?

Thoughts on Afterlife

_____

_____

_____
DATE

☐ Where do I think I go after I physically die?

_____

_____

_____
DATE

☐ Have I shared my beliefs about afterlife and my whereabouts with my loved ones?

_____

_____

_____
DATE

☐ What images, stories, places, or events can I turn to for information and comfort concerning death and what comes afterwards?

_____

_____

_____
DATE

Amy Harwell holds a Masters Degree in Social Service Administration and authored *When Your Friend Gets Cancer: How You Can Help* in 1987. A member of the National Speakers Association, she has addressed over 150 groups in person or through print, radio, and TV from Palm Beach, Florida, to Portland, Oregon.

Amy is committed to:

—inspiring persons living with life-threatening illnesses (cancer, AIDS, heart disease, etc.) and those recovering from a significant loss to *live joyfully in the precious, present moment*

—encouraging caregivers (family, friends, hospice volunteers and staff, Stephen Ministers, etc.) to *approach, not avoid, their loved ones*

—educating professionals (doctors, nurses, therapists, social workers, lawyers, estate planners, chaplains and other clergy) to *evidence empathy, not merely sympathy*

In order to accomplish these goals, Amy founded Joshua's Tent, a not-for-profit organization through which she provides talks, workshops, and retreats on the subjects of living, dying, grieving, and loving.

For additional information, call 1-800-JHS-TENT or write to:

Amy Harwell
Joshua's Tent
325 South Street
Geneva, IL 60134